# Ready® | 5 Writing INSTRUCTION

Vice President of Product Development: Adam Berkin
Editorial: Karen Casey, Anne Cullen, John Ham, Rob Hill, Susan James, Maura Piazza
Design/Production: Jeremy Spiegel and Mark Nodland
Cover Designer: Matthew Pollock
Cover Illustrator: O'Lamar Gibson

ISBN 978-0-7609-9403-0
©2015—Curriculum Associates, LLC
North Billerica, MA 01862

# Acknowledgments

## Passage Credits

"What Is a Planet?" from NASA Mission: Science website, http://missionscience.nasa.gov/nasascience/what_is_a_planet.html.

"Hydroelectric Power" courtesy of the United States Department of the Interior.

"Dances with Animals" by Ellen R. Braff from ASK magazine, March 2009. Copyright © 2009 by Carus Publishing Company. Reproduced with permission. All Cricket Media material is copyright by Carus Publishing Company, d/b/a Cricket media, and/or various authors and illustrators. Any commercial use or distribution of material without permission is strictly prohibited. Please visit http://www.cricketmedia.com/info/licensing2 for licensing and http://www.cricketmedia.com for subscriptions.

"Staying in Touch—All the Time" by Laurie Shinbaum from APPLESEEDS magazine, March 2011. Copyright © 2011 by Carus Publishing Company. Reproduced with permission. All Cricket Media material is copyright by Carus Publishing Company, d/b/a Cricket media, and/or various authors and illustrators. Any commercial use or distribution of material without permission is strictly prohibited. Please visit http://www.cricketmedia.com/info/licensing2 for licensing and http://www.cricketmedia.com for subscriptions.

## Illustration Credits

page viii: O'Lamar Gibson, assisted by Baroka Thompson

page 12: Pronk Media Inc.

page 15: Jeremy Spiegel

page 17: By permission of Steve Breen and Creators Syndicate, Inc.

pages 42, 44: Chandra Ganegoda

page 165: Pronk Media Inc.

pages 100, 102, 104: Ted Hammond/Deborah Wolfe ltd.

pages 73, 74, 75: JT Morrow/Deborah Wolfe ltd.

## Photography Credits

page viii: Ortis/Shutterstock (background)

page x: Giovanni Cancemi/Fotolia

page 10: Toria/Shutterstock (background)

page 10: Alan Dyer, Inc/Visuals Unlimited/Corbis

page 11: NASA

page 13: Johns Hopkins University Applied Physics Laboratory/Southwest Research Institute (JHUAPL/SwRI)

page 14: NASA, ESA, and the Hubble Heritage Team (STScI/AURA)-ESA/Hubble Collaboration (background)

page 32: FoxPictures/Shutterstock

page 42: studio online/Shutterstock (background)

page 44: Finsterbach/Shutterstock

page 45: ankiro/Shutterstock

page 46: Gerhard Seybert/Fotalia

page 90: wizdata/Shutterstock (left)

page 90: michaeljung/Shutterstock (right)

page 120: Bocman1973/Shutterstock

page 130: EcoPrint/Shutterstock

page 130: Danny Alvarez/Shutterstock (eReader)

page 130: huafeng207/Shutterstock (background)

page 131: fivespots/Shutterstock (left)

page 131: rtbilder/Shutterstock (middle)

page 131: Bloom Design/Shutterstock (right)

page 132: rtbilder/Shutterstock (middle)

page 133: mythja/Shutterstock (background)

page 133: anekoho/Shutterstock (left)

page 133: fivespots/Shutterstock (right)

page 134: Leighton Photography & Imaging/Shutterstock (right)

page 134: Vitalii Hulai/Shutterstock (left)

page 135: Debbie C Jackson/Shutterstock

page 135: JONATHAN PLEDGER/Shutterstock (bottom)

page 136: Menno Schaefer/Shutterstock

page 137: Robert L Kothenbeutel/Shutterstock (top)

page 137: Parinya Hirunthitima/Shutterstock (bottom)

page 152: Zurijeta/Shutterstock

page 162: Monkey Business Images/Shutterstock

page 164: James Flint/Shutterstock

page 164: In-Finity/Shutterstock (icons)

page 164: A-R-T/Shutterstock (background)

page 164: Designsstock/Shutterstock (tablet)

page 167: legenda/Shutterstock

# Table of Contents

## Introduction

## Writing

**Standards**

**Theme** Planets

**Assignment** Write a letter to the editor of a kids' science magazine giving your opinion on the decision to call Pluto a dwarf planet.

- **Source 1** What Is a Planet? **Online Article**
- **Source 2** When Is a Planet Not a Planet? **Magazine Feature Article**

W.5.1, W.5.1a, W.5.1b, W.5.1c, W.5.4, W.5.5, W.5.7, W.5.8, W.5.9b , L.5.2a, L.5.6

**Theme** It's Electric

**Assignment** Write an article explaining how hydroelectric plants and wind-powered turbines produce electricity.

- **Source 1** Hydroelectric Power **Informational Brochure**
- **Source 2** Capturing the Wind **Textbook Chapter**

W.5.2, W.5.2a, W.5.2b, W.5.2d, W.5.4, W.5.5, W.5.7, W.5.8, W.5.9b, L.5.1e

**Theme** Legends

**Assignment** Write a legend about a palace guard who recovers a king's stolen crown.

- **Source** Legends **Online Encyclopedia Entry**

W.5.3, W.5.3a, W.5.3b, W.5.3c, W.5.4, W.5.5, W.5.8, W.5.9b, L.5.1c

## In each of the writing lessons, you will move through the following steps.

**Step 1** Study a Mentor Text

**Step 2** Unpack Your Assignment

**Step 3** Find Text Evidence

**Step 4** Organize Your Evidence

**Step 5** Draft

**Step 6** Revise: First Read

**Step 7** Revise: Second Read

**Step 8** Edit for Conventions

## Language Handbook

# Language Handbook *continued*

# Meet Your Writing Buddies

As you move through each lesson, your Ready Writing Buddies are here to help. In each lesson, your buddy is doing the same assignment as you are.

**Luna**

**Hobbies** Time travel; space travel

**Favorites** Doodling

**Hanging Out** Luna and her parents run a time-travel tour guide service known as Infinite Dimensions. Luna can draw a place in her special notebook and then be whisked away to whatever's shown there. Luna never gets tired of traveling around the globe and sometimes even to places that are out of this world!

**Hobbies** Reading; thinking; talking

**Favorites** Making sure everything's perfect

**Hanging Out** Bella hosts a web series named Tool Bella's Cella with her brother, Beau. In the series, Beau and Bella do projects together. They might repair a sink, program a computer, or fix a robot. Bella is always in charge, and the audience loves her for it. She knows exactly what to say and what to do because her heart is always in the right place.

**Bella**

**Olive**

**Hobbies** Yoga; creating art

**Favorites** Designing fliers for a peace rally

**Hanging Out** Olive may be small in size, but has big dreams and she takes action in a big way. With her friends Azul and G.O., Olive's group Rise Over Run has done huge things for her community. But Olive won't stop until the entire world is a better place.

**Sweet T**

**Hobbies** Skateboarding

**Favorites** Jamming out to music; baking

**Hanging Out** Sweet T and his friends, Jake and Pepper Jackie, are the Bake Stars. Together they stir up some serious fun for their web-based cooking show. Sweet T can be a little forgetful, but he's good at math and great at cooking.

**Hobbies** Learning more about computers

**Favorites** Tinkering with Victor the Robot, his amazing invention

**Hanging Out** Beau and his sister, Bella, host a web series called Tool Bella's Cella. Beau can fix anything that's broken, and he's a whiz with a computer. Even though Beau sometimes sounds more robot than human, he's a great friend.

**Beau**

**Azul**

**Hobbies** Soccer; hiking

**Favorites** Helping old ladies cross the street

**Hanging Out** Azul and his friends Olive and G.O. make up a club named Rise Over Run. Azul's role is to lend a helping hand (and it's a big hand) to people in the community. The only thing bigger than Azul's love of nature is the size of his heart.

# Lesson 1
# Writing an Opinion: Letter to the Editor

**W.5.1:** Write opinion pieces on topics or texts, supporting a point of view with reasons and information.

**W.5.7:** Conduct short research projects that use several sources to build knowledge through investigation of different aspects of a topic.

## Sharing Opinions

Sabrina has been reading a new science blog. She loves topics that make her think, especially controversial ones. A recent blog post— a type of online article or essay— was about androids, or robots that act like people. The post described a future in which androids serve humans and do dangerous or unwanted jobs.

Sabrina worried, though, about what might happen if there really were androids. She wanted the other blog readers to think about the dangers, too. To express her opinion, she wrote a response in the Comments section at the end of the blog post. Part of what Sabrina wrote is shown on the tablet below.

A response to a blog post is just one way people express their opinions. Opinions show up in letters to the editor, speeches, debates, and everyday conversation. Well-supported opinions tend to be taken more seriously than those based only on emotions or a lack of information.

4:15 PM     90%

I was fascinated by this post about androids. There would be many good things about having them. As you pointed out, androids could do jobs that are unsafe or boring. But I don't think we should build androids. They might create new problems.

For instance, today some people have trouble finding jobs. What if androids did all the work? Machines already do the jobs of bank tellers, factory workers, and supermarket . . .

## What Is Opinion Writing?

Opinion writing expresses a writer's point of view—his or her thoughts, feelings, or beliefs—about a topic. The writer supports this opinion by presenting reasons for it, as well as relevant evidence, such as facts and details, to explain and support each reason.

KEY FEATURES | **Opinion Writing**

- an introduction that gets readers interested in the topic and presents a clear opinion statement
- paragraphs that provide logically ordered reasons supported by evidence
- linking words, phrases, and clauses that clearly connect the opinion to reasons, and reasons to evidence
- a conclusion that restates the opinion and leaves readers with something to think about

## Steps for Writing

On the following pages, you'll learn the steps for writing your own letter to the editor.

**The Research Path**

| | |
|---|---|
| **Step 1** Study a Mentor Text | **Step 5** Draft Your Letter |
| **Step 2** Unpack Your Assignment | **Step 6** Revise: First Read |
| **Step 3** Find Text Evidence | **Step 7** Revise: Second Read |
| **Step 4** Organize Your Evidence | **Step 8** Edit for Conventions |

# Step 1 Study a Mentor Text

Before you write your letter to the editor, you'll study a model. First, read to understand what it's about. Then reread to understand how it was written.

**As you reread the Mentor Text, do the numbered activities. They'll help you understand the key features of a letter to the editor.**

**MENTOR TEXT: Letter to the Editor**

## Space Tourism Can Wait

1    A recent article in your magazine reported that space tourism is becoming popular for private citizens in this country and around the world. Many people love the idea of touring outer space—and the possibility is exciting to think about. However, space tourism comes with huge costs to people here on Earth and to our already struggling environment. I strongly believe that space tourism is not worth the price at this time.

2    Why do I say this? First of all, the actual monetary cost of space travel is incredibly high. For example, a short trip into orbit around Earth can cost around $200,000. A trip all the way to the International Space Station is even costlier, topping out at around $20 million for just one person. According to my research, seven space tourists have already made that trip, and one person has done it twice. That adds up to about $160 million! Private citizens certainly are free to spend their money however they'd like, but just imagine what would happen if, instead, they each put $20 million into improving schools, feeding the hungry, or providing low-cost health care for the poor. Instead of just pursuing their own dreams, the wealthy could improve the lives of many people not as fortunate as they are. That might not be nearly as fun as a trip into space, but it might be a lot more fulfilling.

**1 Opinion Statement  Draw a dashed line** below the sentence that states the writer's opinion.

**2 Reasons** Paragraphs 2–4 each give a reason supporting the writer's opinion. **Underline** each reason. **Label** them **R-1**, **R-2**, and **R-3**.

**3 Evidence**  In paragraph 2, the writer provides facts to support his reason. Name two of the facts he provides.

_____

_____

_____

_____

3    Second, there are no guarantees that space travel is safe for the general public. As the website Theweek.com points out, "when dealing with rockets, there's always a chance something will explode." The history of space travel shows that such disasters, although rare, can definitely occur. Moreover, the government has no laws about who can go into space. The only rules that space-tourism companies have are that space tourists must be in good health, and people under the age of 14 must be accompanied by an adult. Otherwise, space tourism is open to anyone who can afford it. These rules are not strict enough. Professional astronauts go through long years of training before they are allowed to fly into space. There is little doubt that astronauts are better equipped than the general public to handle any dangers that might arise during the flight.

4    Finally, the monetary cost of space tourism is nothing compared to the price our planet might pay. Specifically, the rockets used to propel tourists into space produce air pollution—and lots of it. Some experts say that launching a thousand space flights a year would produce as much pollution as all other air travel combined. At the moment, only a handful of private citizens travel into space each year, but those numbers are increasing. As a result, climate change is on the rise, too. We are already seeing melting glaciers, changing weather patterns, and dwindling food supplies in some parts of the world. Such changes have a greater effect on the people of poor nations than those in rich nations, and it is in the rich nations where our current space tourists live. In other words, space tourism would only intensify the threat to our planet and its people, especially those living in poor countries.

5    There's no question that space tourism is an exciting idea. However, it needs to become less expensive and a lot safer for people and the planet. If and when that happens, space tourism might be a great way for private citizens to participate in exploring the next frontier. But until we learn to take better care of our own planet and the people who live on it, space tourism can wait.

*Hakan Jackson*
*Columbus, Ohio*

**4  Linking Words, Phrases & Clauses**
In paragraph 3, the writer uses a clause, a group of words that has a subject and a predicate, to connect a reason with supporting evidence. **Draw a box** around that clause.

**5  Evidence**  Explain why the writer includes information from experts in paragraph 4.

_____

_____

_____

_____

**6  Conclusion  Draw a dashed line** below the two sentences that restate the writer's opinion.

W.5.4: Produce clear and coherent writing in which the development and organization are appropriate to task, purpose, and audience.

# Step 2  Unpack Your Assignment

FOCUS Identify Task, Purpose, and Audience

Before you begin writing, you should read your assignment carefully and plan your work. Begin by identifying your task, purpose, and audience.

- Your **task** is what you need to do to complete the assignment.

- Your **purpose** is your reason for writing, such as to entertain, to inform, or to express an opinion.

- Your **audience** is the person or group that will read your finished piece.

## Modeled Instruction

Hakan Jackson, who wrote "Space Tourism Can Wait" on pages 2–3, was given the assignment below. He read it carefully and marked up some important details.

**Read Hakan's assignment. Then read the points in his Think Aloud, which tell how he identified his task, purpose, and audience.**

### HAKAN'S Assignment

A popular science magazine recently featured an article about space tourism. According to the article, wealthy citizens can now travel to the International Space Station. Many people are excited about space tourism, but others think it's a bad idea. Write a letter to the editor giving your opinion on whether space tourism should be allowed.

In your letter to the editor:

- State your opinion about whether space tourism should be allowed or not.

- Provide logically ordered reasons to support your opinion.

- Support your reasons with facts and details.

### Think Aloud

- **Audience**  I'm writing in response to an article in a science magazine. Although I'm writing a letter "to the editor," that really just means my letter will be published in the front of the magazine for all the readers to see. So my readers are people who read this magazine and enjoy reading about science.

- **Purpose**  I'm writing to share my opinion about space tourism. I'll need to explain my reasons for holding that opinion. If I can back up my reasons with strong facts and details, I might convince my readers to agree with me.

- **Task**  My task is to write a letter to the editor that gives my opinion about whether space tourism should be allowed. The phrase *logically ordered reasons* means I'll need to figure out the best way to organize my information. The phrase *facts and details* tells me I'll have to find reliable evidence to back up my opinion.

## Guided Practice

**Now it's your turn to write a letter to the editor. Read Your Assignment carefully. Then complete the activities, using the Hints for help.**

### Your Assignment

A magazine for kids who like science recently published an article about the decision in 2006 to reclassify Pluto as a "dwarf planet." At the time, many people disagreed with the decision, but many others accepted it. Arguments about the decision continue to this day. Write a letter to the editor of the magazine, giving your opinion on whether the decision to reclassify Pluto was correct.

**To prepare to write your letter to the editor, you will read the following:**

- What Is a Planet? *pages 10–13*
- When Is a Planet Not a Planet? *pages 14–17*

**In your letter to the editor:**

- State your opinion about whether the decision was correct or not.
- Provide logically ordered reasons to support your opinion.
- Support your reasons with facts and details from the source texts.

*Hi, I'm Luna, and I'm also going to be doing this assignment.*

**1 Audience** **Draw a box** around the words that help you identify your audience. How does an understanding of your audience affect what you will write?

_____

_____

**HINT** Remember that a letter to the editor is not meant just for the editor to read.

**2 Purpose** **Draw a dashed line** under your purpose for writing. Then describe it in your own words.

_____

_____

**HINT** Why do people usually write letters to the editor?

**3 Task** **Circle** the type of writing you will do. Then **underline** a key word or phrase in each bulleted item that describes what your writing must include.

**HINT** What are the key features of opinion writing?

**Turn and Talk** Why is it important to organize your ideas logically?

# The Research Path
## Writing from Sources

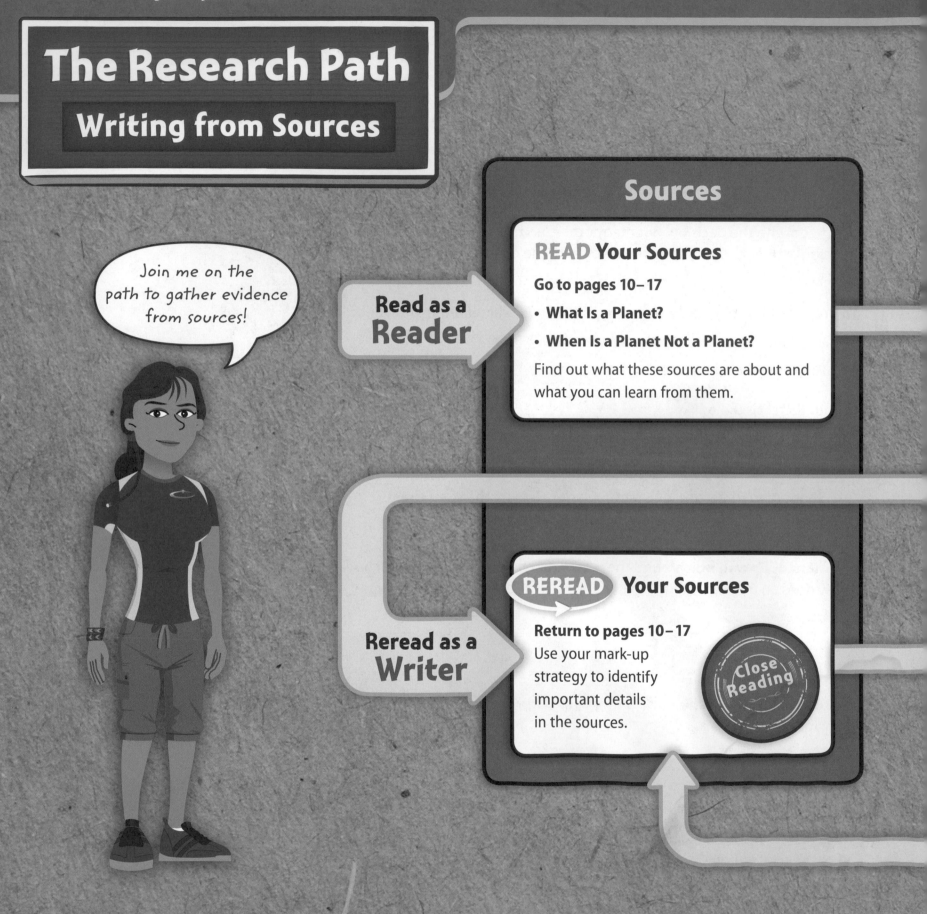

Join me on the path to gather evidence from sources!

**Sources**

**READ Your Sources**

**Go to pages 10–17**

- **What Is a Planet?**
- **When Is a Planet Not a Planet?**

Find out what these sources are about and what you can learn from them.

**Read as a Reader**

**REREAD Your Sources**

**Return to pages 10–17**

Use your mark-up strategy to identify important details in the sources.

Close Reading

**Reread as a Writer**

## REVIEW Your Assignment

**Return to page 5**
Reread your task to identify the types of information you will need to include in your letter to the editor.

## Text Evidence

### FIND Text Evidence

**Go to pages 8–9**
Learn how to mark important details so you can find them quickly later on.

## THINK It Through

**Go to pages 18–19**
Complete the activities to help you connect the ideas in the sources to your assignment.

## ORGANIZE Your Evidence

**Go to pages 20–21**
Use a chart to group your reasons and supporting evidence so that you're ready to write.

**Need More Information?**
Yes, see Write Time, page 19

**Begin Writing!**
Go to pages 22–23

**W.5.8:** . . . gather relevant information from print . . . sources. . . .

# Step 3 Find Text Evidence

Before you can form an opinion, you need to first consider both sides of the issue. You should look for details both for and against the decision to reclassify Pluto.

Details that support an idea are called **pros**. Details that are against an idea are called **cons**. As you reread the source texts on pages 10–17, mark details supporting the decision to reclassify Pluto with a **P**, for *pro,* and details against the decision with a **C**, for *con*. Then you'll be able to review the details when it's time to form your opinion.

## Modeled Instruction

Luna underlined details and marked up the text as she read the source text, "When Is a Planet Not a Planet?"

**Read the text and Luna's Think Aloud to learn more about the reading and mark-up strategies she used.**

From **"When Is a Planet Not a Planet?"** *page 17*

C    . . . One IAU member said that Pluto should stay a planet "partly for historical reasons," and others agreed. Members of the public, including angry schoolchildren, wrote the IAU demanding that Pluto stay a planet. New Mexico lawmakers even passed a bill saying that Pluto was still a planet. Even if other Kuiper Belt Objects are dwarf planets, they said, leave Pluto alone.

But supporters of the change argue that historical reasons shouldn't get in the way of science. After all, people believed for centuries that the planets and the sun orbit Earth, but scientists eventually discovered the truth: Earth and the other planets orbit the sun. In a similar way, new discoveries led scientists to question the historical view of what a planet is. The new definition isn't perfect, say its supporters, but it's more accurate than the old way of thinking.

**Think Aloud**

● Let's see . . . the writer says that some IAU scientists said Pluto should stay a planet for "historical reasons." In other words, those scientists were against the decision to reclassify Pluto as a dwarf planet. So, even some members of the group making the decision thought it was a mistake! That seems like evidence that the IAU made the wrong decision. I'll mark this detail with a C, for *con*.

● Now the writer tells what supporters of the IAU's decision think: Just because a belief has been around for centuries doesn't mean it's right. Astronomers discovered new facts about the solar system, and these facts led to a new definition of what a planet is. This is evidence that the IAU made the right decision in reclassifying Pluto. I'll mark these sentences with a P, for *pro*.

Read the following excerpt from "What Is a Planet?" Then complete the activities, using the Hints for help.

From **"What Is a Planet?"** *pages 12–13*

To clear an orbit, a planet must be big enough to pull neighboring objects into the planet itself or sling-shot them around the planet and shoot them off into outer space. According to the IAU, Pluto does not meet this third requirement but is now in a new class of objects called "dwarf planets." It is this third part of the definition that has sparked debate.

**The Problem for Pluto**

The problem for Pluto is the fact that its orbit is in the Kuiper Belt along with 43 other known KBOs. There are possibly billions of objects in the Kuiper Belt that have not been cataloged yet. Scientists have even found 8 KBOs between Neptune and Pluto. Some scientists view the new definition as unclear. Exactly how much does Pluto have to "clear" from its neighborhood to be considered a planet? And how much has Pluto already influenced its own neighborhood since the planet formed?

**1** Does the first underlined sentence suggest the IAU's decision was correct or incorrect? **Mark** it with a P or a C. Then explain why you marked it that way.

_____

_____

_____

**HINT** If the third requirement is accurate, what does that say about the IAU's decision?

**2** Should you mark the second underlined sentence with a P or a C? **Mark** the sentence, and then explain your choice.

_____

_____

_____

**HINT** Read the sentences around the underlined sentence for more information.

**Turn and Talk** How will marking up your sources in this way help you keep track of information and develop your own opinion?

# WHAT IS A PLANET?

**From The National Aeronautics and Space Administration (NASA)**

1     Technically, there was never a scientific definition of the term *planet* before 2006. When the Greeks observed the sky thousands of years ago, they discovered objects that acted differently than stars. These points of light seemed to wander around the sky throughout the year. We get the term *planet* from the Greek word *planētēs,* meaning "wanderer."

**For all of human history, five planets have been easily visible with the naked eye: Mercury, Venus, Mars, Jupiter, and Saturn.**

## Telescopes Add to Our Knowledge

2     In the 1600s, scientists began to use telescopes to view our solar system. As technology got better, scientists discovered more planets orbiting our Sun, such as Uranus in 1781, Neptune in 1846, and Pluto in 1930. Then, in 1991, advances in telescope technology enabled scientists to discover many more objects in a disk-shaped cloud beyond Pluto called the Kuiper (KYE per) Belt. These objects were classified as Kuiper Belt Objects (KBOs), partly because they are smaller than Pluto. This classification of KBO seemed to work fine as long as objects weren't bigger than Pluto.

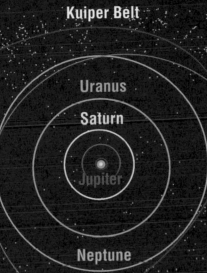

## Outer Solar System

**Kuiper Belt**

**Uranus**

**Saturn**

**Jupiter**

**Neptune**

Eris

**Pluto**

Some scientists believe that if Pluto remains classified as a planet, then the dozens of Kuiper Belt Objects (KBOs) orbiting our Sun would also be classified as planets. Our solar system would have the 9 original planets, an additional 43 KBOs, and more as they are cataloged.

## Eris, the Goddess of Discord

3    It was the recent discovery of an object larger than Pluto within the Kuiper Belt that changed everything. Is this object, now named Eris, our 10th planet, since it is larger than Pluto? This discovery and the naming of this new object prompted the International Astronomical Union (IAU) to discuss a scientific definition for the term *planet*. What if Eris is given planet status? Then our solar system could grow to dozens of planets as more and more Kuiper Belt Objects are discovered. Try remembering all those planet names. But if Eris is not a planet, then is Pluto still a planet?

### The New Definition

4     Astronomers of the IAU voted on and passed the first scientific definition of a planet in August 2006. According to this new definition, an object must meet three criteria in order to be classified as a planet.

• First, it must orbit the Sun.

• Second, it must be big enough for gravity to squash it into a round ball.

• And third, it must have cleared other objects out of the way in its orbital neighborhood.

5     To clear an orbit, a planet must be big enough to pull neighboring objects into the planet itself or sling-shot them around the planet and shoot them off into outer space. According to the IAU, Pluto does not meet this third requirement but is now in a new class of objects called "dwarf planets." It is this third part of the definition that has sparked debate.

## The ③ Criteria for Being a Planet

**①** A planet must orbit the Sun.

**②** A planet must be big enough for gravity to squash it into a ball.

**③** A planet must clear other objects from its orbital path. This can be done in one of two ways:

The planet pulls the objects into itself.

The planet sling-shots the objects out of its orbital path and into outer space.

## The Problem for Pluto

6    The problem for Pluto is the fact that its orbit is in the Kuiper Belt along with 43 other known KBOs. There are possibly billions of objects in the Kuiper Belt that have not been cataloged yet. Scientists have even found 8 KBOs between Neptune and Pluto. Some scientists view the new definition as unclear. Exactly how much does Pluto have to "clear" from its neighborhood to be considered a planet? And how much has Pluto already influenced its own neighborhood since the planet formed? These and other questions have been raised in response to the IAU's definition of a planet.

7    Consider this: Pluto crosses into Neptune's orbit, but Neptune is still classified as a planet. This is because of the orbits of Pluto and Neptune and the fact that they never get closer to each other than 17 AU. (1 AU = distance from Earth to the Sun.) Pluto may cross orbits with many other Kuiper Belt Objects, but how close do these objects get to Pluto? How close do objects have to get to Pluto to be considered "in" Pluto's neighborhood?

## Journey to the Edge

8    NASA's *New Horizons* spacecraft is speeding toward the edge of the solar system on its mission to Pluto. Launched in January 2006, it will not be until July 2015 that we will reach Pluto. It will swing past Jupiter for a gravity boost and scientific studies in February 2007, and reach Pluto and its moon, Charon, in July 2015. Then, as part of an extended mission, the spacecraft would head deeper into the Kuiper Belt to study one or more of the icy mini-worlds in that vast region, at least a billion miles beyond Neptune's orbit. Sending a spacecraft on this long journey will help us answer basic questions about the surface properties, geology, interior makeup, and atmospheres on these bodies.

Artist's concept of the *New Horizons* spacecraft's planned encounter with Pluto in 2015

# WHEN IS a Planet NOT a Planet?

## ANSWER: When It's a Dwarf Planet . . . Maybe    BY DANIEL SANTOS

1    In 2005 our solar system had nine planets. In 2007 there were only eight: Pluto was no longer considered a planet. What happened? No, an asteroid didn't destroy Pluto, and it didn't escape from the solar system. Instead, a group called the International Astronomical Union (IAU), which has the authority to name and classify objects in space, decided in August 2006 that Pluto was not a planet. Pluto, they said, was something else: a dwarf planet.

2    Many scientists and nonscientists agreed with Pluto's reclassification—but not all. Some fought to keep Pluto a planet. So what was the fight about?

## Defining a Planet . . . for the First Time

3    To understand the conflict, it helps to know a startling fact: Before 2006 scientists had no official definition of a planet. If an object was round and moved around the sun, it was a planet. When Pluto was discovered in 1930, scientists knew it met these criteria, so they called it a planet. But over time, scientists realized that Pluto was unusual. It was extremely small and made mostly of ice. It also had a strange orbit, as the diagrams on the next page show. But it was round and it moved around the sun, so it stayed a planet.

4    This situation went on for nearly 70 years. But in the 1990s two discoveries made astronomers start rethinking Pluto's status. First, they learned Pluto orbited in a vast sea of rock and ice debris called the Kuiper (KYE per) Belt. Second, they found other objects in the Kuiper Belt very much like Pluto— other balls of rock and ice. One such ball, now called Eris, was larger than Pluto. Now Pluto, the oddball of the planets, had close relatives.

5    Astronomers had a dilemma. If they called these Pluto-like objects planets, then the number of planets in the solar system could skyrocket to 50 or more. It would become almost impossible to memorize the names of all the planets. But did it actually make sense to group Pluto and its relatives with the other planets? Or should these rock-and-ice balls have their own group? Faced with these questions, many astronomers began wishing for a firmer definition of the word planet. They looked to the IAU to provide one.

## Reaching a Definition

6    During the 2000s the IAU worked on developing a definition of a *planet* that its members could vote on. After years of work, on August 24, 2006, the IAU voted on and approved a definition. According to the definition, a planet must (1) orbit the sun, (2) be massive enough for its own gravity to have pulled it into a sphere, and (3) have cleared other objects from its orbital neighborhood. Pluto fails to meet the third criterion: It shares its neighborhood with far too many chunks of rock and ice. So, Pluto isn't a planet—it's a dwarf planet.

7    Right after the vote, many astronomers objected to the new definition. Alan Stern, head of the *New Horizons* mission to Pluto, called it "awful" and "sloppy science." The website Newscientist.com declared, "It appears likely that the definition will not be widely adopted by astronomers for everyday use." Within days of the vote, 304 astronomers had signed a petition protesting the IAU's definition. Those same astronomers also declared that the voting process had been deeply flawed.

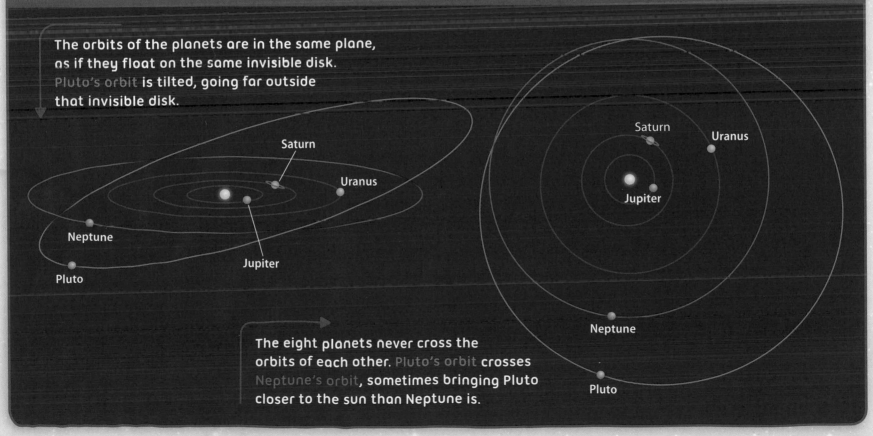

## Two Views of Pluto's Orbit

The orbits of the planets are in the same plane, as if they float on the same invisible disk. Pluto's orbit is tilted, going far outside that invisible disk.

Saturn
Uranus
Neptune
Jupiter
Pluto

Saturn
Uranus
Jupiter
Neptune
Pluto

The eight planets never cross the orbits of each other. Pluto's orbit crosses Neptune's orbit, sometimes bringing Pluto closer to the sun than Neptune is.

## Clearing the Neighborhood

8    The 304 astronomers who protested the definition focused on the third criterion—that a planet must have "cleared the neighborhood around its orbit." But what does "clear the neighborhood" mean? How big is the neighborhood? How clear must a planet make its orbit? Earth, Mars, Jupiter, and Neptune all share their orbits with thousands of asteroids, but no one claims they aren't planets. Also, asked protesters, why does it matter that Pluto's neighborhood is full of smaller objects? If a body goes around the sun and is round, why isn't that enough? As Alan Stern put it, planets "are what they are, independent of what they orbit near." Until the IAU revises the definition to answer these and other questions, the protesters declared, Pluto should stay a planet.

> ### The Kuiper Belt Dwarf Planets . . .
> - are about the size of Pluto or smaller.
> - are made mostly of ice and rock.
> - share their orbits with many small chunks of rock and ice.
> - have tilted orbits that cross the orbits of planets, other dwarf planets, or both.

9    But the definition's supporters argue that the third criterion is accurate enough. True, Earth, Mars, Jupiter, and Neptune share their orbits with asteroids. But those planets have cleared their orbits far more successfully than Pluto has. What's more, they say, the orbits of Pluto and the similar Kuiper Belt Objects have more in common with each other than with the orbits of the eight planets. It just makes sense to split the solar system into two groups. Astronomer Mike Brown, who discovered many Kuiper Belt Objects, put it this way: "The precise definition . . . may be a tad unclear, but the concept is absolutely rock solid with absolutely no room for doubt about which objects do and do not belong." In other words, if you say "planet," everyone knows you mean the eight planets. If you say "dwarf planet," everyone knows you mean the other round objects orbiting the sun. The definitions aren't perfect, but they're very useful.

## Problems with the Vote

10    Critics of the IAU's decision had another complaint: Not enough IAU members were allowed to vote on the new definition. In 2006 about 10,000 astronomers belonged to the IAU. Of those, fewer than 500 voted. Why so few? Because only members who are in the room when a vote is held can vote. If IAU members were allowed to vote by e-mail, say some astronomers, the definition of planet might not have passed. For many, the small number of voters is a problem. Astronomer David Weintraub, author of the book *Is Pluto a Planet?*, said, "I'm not convinced that the folks who were at the meeting represented well the larger community."

## History or Science?

11      There was another objection to Pluto's reclassification. Pluto's identity as a planet wasn't just a matter of science. It was also a matter of history. After all, Pluto had been a planet for more than 70 years. People had grown used to the idea. Textbooks and museums would have to change what they said. One IAU member said that Pluto should stay a planet "partly for historical reasons," and others agreed. Members of the public, including angry schoolchildren, wrote the IAU demanding that Pluto stay a planet. New Mexico lawmakers even passed a bill saying that Pluto was still a planet. Even if other Kuiper Belt Objects are dwarf planets, they said, leave Pluto alone.

12      But supporters of the change argue that historical reasons shouldn't get in the way of science. After all, people believed for centuries that the planets and the sun orbit Earth, but scientists eventually discovered the truth: Earth and the other planets orbit the sun. In a similar way, new discoveries led scientists to question the historical view of what a planet is. The new definition isn't perfect, say its supporters, but it's more accurate than the old way of thinking. In spite of "historical reasons," Pluto must go.

By permission of Steve Breen and Creators Syndicate, Inc.

This editorial cartoon was published right after Pluto's reclassification as a dwarf planet. Many cartoonists seemed to feel sorry for Pluto.

## What's Next?

13      By now, people are used to the idea that Pluto isn't a planet, even if not everyone agrees with that idea. But is the definition of planet settled? Probably not. First of all, the IAU's definition applies only to objects in our own solar system. But astronomers have discovered huge, round objects circling distant stars. Most people would agree these objects are planets, but they aren't covered by the definition. Shouldn't a good definition of planet work beyond our own solar system? Furthermore, astronomers have even found some solid round objects in space that don't orbit any stars at all. Are they planets?

14      No matter what happens to Pluto, two things are certain: Science will keep making new discoveries, and scientists and nonscientists alike will argue about what each new discovery means.

## Think It Through

**Use details from your sources to complete the following activities. Your answers will help you write your letter to the editor.**

**1** Based on the information you've read, do you think the decision to reclassify Pluto as a dwarf planet was correct or incorrect? Write your opinion statement below.

_____

_____

> **HINT** As you read the sources, what side of the debate seemed to have the most convincing reasons and evidence?

**2** List three reasons supporting your opinion about the decision to reclassify Pluto. The example below shows how you can combine related details into a single reason.

> **HINT** A *reason* is a general statement that can be supported with facts, details, or examples.

**Example:**

Detail: Pluto is made of rock and ice like other Kuiper Belt Objects.

Detail: Pluto's orbit is tilted compared with the other planets' orbits.

Reason: Pluto is too different from the other planets.

Reason: _____

_____

Reason: _____

_____

Reason: _____

_____

**3** On the lines below, write an opinion statement that is **opposite** to the one you wrote for activity 1.

_____

**4** List three reasons that support the opinion statement you wrote in activity 3. Look back at the example in activity 2 to show how you can combine related details into a single reason.

**HINT** Look back at the details you marked with a P or C for ideas that support the other side.

Reason 1: _____

_____

Reason 2: _____

_____

Reason 3: _____

_____

**5** Now that you have completed activities 3 and 4, do you still hold the opinion that you wrote down in activity 1? Or has your opinion changed?

**HINT** Use the details you marked and the notes you made to help you develop each reason.

_____

_____

**6** Complete the frame below to express your opinion and reasons in one statement.

**HINT** Use your responses to activities 1 and 2 (or activities 3 and 4) to help you complete the frame.

I believe that the decision to reclassify Pluto as a dwarf planet was _____

because [reason 1] _____ ,

[reason 2] _____ ,

and [reason 3] _____ .

## Write Time ✏️

Return to your sources to identify facts and details that support each of your reasons. Mark evidence for each reason with the code R-1, R-2, or R-3.

# Step 4  Organize Your Evidence

**W.5.5:** With guidance and support from peers and adults, develop and strengthen writing as needed by planning. . . .

**W.5.8:** . . . summarize or paraphrase information in notes. . . .

**FOCUS**  Plan Your Letter to the Editor

Now that you've formed your opinion and identified your supporting reasons, it's time to plan your letter to the editor.

Each of your reasons helps explain why your audience should agree with your opinion. In the same way, evidence—the facts and details you marked in the sources—helps explain each reason. As you write your letter, each reason and its supporting evidence will make up one paragraph.

## Modeled Instruction

To organize her reasons and supporting evidence, Luna created the chart below.

**Look at Luna's opinion, her first reason, and the detail that supports her reason. Find another fact or detail in the passage that supports this reason. Underline it and add it to the chart.**

From **"What Is a Planet?"** *page 13*

Exactly how much does Pluto have to "clear" from its neighborhood to be considered a planet? And how much has Pluto already influenced its own neighborhood since the planet formed?

Consider this: Pluto crosses into Neptune's orbit, but Neptune is still classified as a planet. This is because of the orbits of Pluto and Neptune and the fact that they never get closer to each other than 17 AU. (1 AU = distance from Earth to the Sun.) Pluto may cross orbits with many other Kuiper Belt Objects, but how close do these objects get to Pluto? How close do objects have to get to Pluto to be considered "in" Pluto's neighborhood?

**Luna's Chart**

| My Opinion: The IAU made the wrong decision in reclassifying Pluto as a dwarf planet. | |
|---|---|
| **Reason 1** The third part of the IAU's definition is vague. | **Evidence** • It doesn't say how much an object has to "clear" from its neighborhood to be a planet. • _____ _____ _____ |

## 🐾 Guided Practice

Luna's classmate Beau has the opposite opinion. Help him continue filling in his chart by completing the activities. Use the Hints for help.

From **"When Is a Planet Not a Planet?"** *page 16*

But the definition's supporters argue that the third criterion is accurate enough. <u>True, Earth, Mars, Jupiter, and Neptune share their orbits with asteroids. But those planets have cleared their orbits far more successfully than Pluto has.</u> What's more, they say, the orbits of Pluto and the similar Kuiper Belt Objects have more in common with each other than with the orbits of the eight planets. It just makes sense to split the solar system into two groups.

**Beau's Chart**

| My Opinion: The IAU made the right decision in reclassifying Pluto as a dwarf planet. | |
|---|---|
| **Reason 1** The IAU's definition of "planet" is accurate enough. | **Evidence** • Earth, Mars, Jupiter, and Neptune have been more successful at clearing their orbits than Pluto has. <br><br> • _____ _____ _____ |

**1** Find an additional detail in the excerpt that supports Beau's reason. **Underline** it, and **add** it to the chart. Explain why it supports the reason.

_____

_____

_____

> **HINT** What other information supports the idea that Pluto should be in a different group?

**2** Explain how Beau might turn these notes into one or more paragraphs of his letter to the editor.

_____

_____

_____

_____

> **HINT** Look back at the organization of the Mentor Text.

💬 **Turn and Talk** Discuss what questions you can ask yourself to help identify the evidence that is important enough to include in your chart.

### Write Time ✏️

In your own chart, record the reasons for your opinion and then organize the evidence you identified to support each reason.

# Step 5 Draft Your Letter

W.5.1: Write opinion pieces on topics or texts, supporting a point of view with reasons and information.

W.5.1a: Introduce a topic or text clearly, state an opinion, and create an organizational structure in which ideas are logically grouped to support the writer's purpose.

FOCUS  Write an Introduction

**Read this chart to learn more about the main parts of a letter to the editor. You can refer back to this information as you write your draft.**

## Parts of a Letter to the Editor

### INTRODUCTION

Introduces the topic and clearly states your opinion

A strong introduction grabs the readers' attention and makes them want to read more. It should:

- **Introduce the topic** by telling what your letter is in response to and offering an initial thought or reaction.
- **Explain the issue** you will be writing about.
- **State your opinion** clearly so that readers understand your point of view.

### BODY

Supports your opinion with reasons and evidence

Each paragraph or section of the body should develop one reason that supports your opinion. Remember to:

- Present your reasons in a **logical order**, such as by order of importance. Start or end with the reason that seems strongest.
- Support your reasons with evidence by including **facts and details**.
- Connect ideas with **linking words, phrases, and clauses** to help them flow together smoothly.

### CONCLUSION

Restates your opinion and tells why it matters

A strong conclusion leaves readers with a good understanding of your point of view. You should:

- Briefly **restate your opinion** and summarize your reasons.
- End with a strong statement that leaves your readers with **something to think about**.

## Draft Your INTRODUCTION

Practice writing the parts of an introduction. Study each example from the Mentor Text. Then try writing each part of your introduction.

**INTRODUCTION**

BODY

CONCLUSION

### Introduce the Topic

| Mentor Text | A recent article in your magazine reported that space tourism is becoming popular for private citizens in this country and around the world. Many people love the idea of touring outer space—and the possibility is exciting to think about. |
|---|---|
| Your Letter | |

**HINT** What made people really notice what the IAU had been discussing in the 2000s?

### Explain the Issue

| Mentor Text | However, space tourism comes with huge costs to people here on Earth and to our already struggling environment. |
|---|---|
| Your Letter | |

**HINT** How did people react to the change in Pluto's status?

### State Your Opinion

| Mentor Text | I strongly believe that space tourism is not worth the price at this time. |
|---|---|
| Your Letter | |

**HINT** Words such as *think*, *agree with*, or *believe* can signal an opinion.

**Turn and Talk** Discuss why crafting a good introduction is important when writing a letter to the editor.

### Write Time

Use your ideas from this page to draft your introduction. Then begin drafting your body paragraphs.

**W.5.1b:** Provide logically ordered reasons that are supported by facts and details.

FOCUS Use Strong Evidence

## Draft Your BODY

Each of your body paragraphs should begin with a reason that supports your opinion. Use strong evidence, including facts and details to develop each reason.

- A **fact** is a specific kind of detail that can be proven. Facts include **numbers**, **dates**, and **definitions**.

- **Details** provide additional information to help your audience understand your ideas. Details include **facts**, **descriptions**, and **examples**.

**Strong evidence** is specific, reliable, and closely related to the idea it supports.

INTRODUCTION

BODY

CONCLUSION

## Modeled Instruction

**Read the excerpt from "Space Tourism Can Wait." Complete the activities to understand what makes a strong piece of evidence.**

### From MENTOR TEXT page 3

Finally, the monetary cost of space tourism is nothing compared to the price our planet might pay. Specifically, the rockets used to propel tourists into space produce air pollution—and lots of it. Some experts say that launching a thousand space flights a year would produce as much pollution as all other air travel combined. At the moment, only a handful of private citizens travel into space each year, but those numbers are increasing. As a result, climate change is on the rise, too. We are already seeing melting glaciers, changing weather patterns, and dwindling food supplies in some parts of the world. Such changes have a greater effect on the people of poor nations than those in rich nations, and it is in the rich nations where our current space tourists live. In other words, space tourism would only intensify the threat to our planet and its people, especially those living in poor countries.

**1** What are two important details in the excerpt that support the reason in the first underlined sentence?

_____

_____

**2** Read the second underlined sentence. What makes this example a strong piece of evidence?

_____

_____

**3** What makes the details in the third underlined sentence strong evidence?

_____

_____

Luna used the notes in her chart to write the draft below. Now she wants to support her reasons by adding additional facts and details.

**Read Luna's notes and draft. Complete the activities, using the Hints for help.**

### Luna's Chart

| My Opinion: The IAU made the wrong decision in reclassifying Pluto as a dwarf planet. | |
|---|---|
| **Reason 1** The third part of the IAU's definition is vague. | **Evidence** <br>• It doesn't say how much an object has to "clear" from its neighborhood to be a planet. <br>• Even though Neptune hasn't cleared Pluto from its orbit, Neptune is still called a planet. <br>• Earth, Mars, and Jupiter share their orbits with asteroids, but they are called planets. |

### Luna's Draft

One reason why I think the IAU made the wrong decision is that the third part of the definition of "planet" is vague. For example, the third part says a planet must have cleared objects from its neighborhood. In addition, some objects in our solar system haven't fully cleared their neighborhoods, but people still call those objects planets. Finally, people other than me also think the third part of the definition is too vague.

**4** Luna needs to add a detail to the underlined sentence to better support her reason. What detail should she add? Explain your answer.

_____

_____

> **HINT** The sentence tells only what the third part of the definition says.

**5** Read the sentence with the dashed underline. Explain how Luna can make the evidence in that sentence stronger.

_____

_____

> **HINT** Reread Luna's notes and compare them to the sentences in her draft.

**6** **Draw a wavy line** below a sentence in Luna's draft that has weak evidence. Explain why it is weak.

_____

_____

> **HINT** Reread page 24 to review what counts as strong evidence.

**Turn and Talk** How can you figure out whether a piece of evidence is strong?

### Write Time

Finish drafting the body of your letter to the editor. Then draft a conclusion using the tips from the chart on page 22 for help.

# Step 6 Revise: First Read

**W.5.4:** Produce clear and coherent writing in which the development and organization are appropriate to task, purpose, and audience.

**W.5.5:** With guidance and support from peers and adults, develop and strengthen writing as needed by . . . revising. . . .

**FOCUS** Ideas and Elaboration

As you revise, use your Opinion Writing Checklist to check your writing. Work through the checklist, one line at a time. Reread the related parts of your letter to the editor to decide whether you did your best possible work for each trait described. In this step, you will check your letter for two of the traits in the categories of Ideas and Elaboration.

## Modeled Instruction

The Mentor Text writer, Hakan Jackson, used the same checklist to evaluate his draft.

**Read his Think Aloud to see how he checks his letter to the editor.**

### MENTOR TEXT Draft

There are no guarantees that space travel is safe for the public. There is always the risk of an accident. And, there are no laws about who can go into space. The only rules are that space tourists must be in good health, and people under age 14 must be accompanied by an adult. Otherwise, space tourism is open to anyone who can afford it.

Space tourism is a bad idea. The rockets used to propel tourists into space produce air pollution— and lots of it. Some experts say that launching a thousand space flights a year would produce as much pollution as all other air travel combined. At the moment, only a handful of private citizens travel into space each year, but their numbers are increasing. As a result, climate change is on the rise, too. We are already seeing melting glaciers, changing weather patterns, and dwindling food supplies in some parts of the world.

### Think Aloud

● **Ideas**  Do I clearly state my reasons in each paragraph? In the first paragraph, I clearly state my reason: There are no guarantees that space travel is safe for the public. So, I'm good there.

But I start the next paragraph by saying "Space tourism is a bad idea." That's an opinion, not a reason. The point of this paragraph is that space tourism could hurt planet Earth. So, I'll delete that sentence and replace it with the following reason: "The monetary cost of space tourism is nothing compared to the price our planet might pay."

● **Elaboration**  In the first paragraph, do I include enough facts and details to support my reason? My reason is that space travel might not be safe for the public. I support it with two facts: There is a risk of an accident, and there are no laws about who can go into space. That's good. And, I develop the fact about the lack of laws with details about who cannot go into space. That's good.

But my audience needs to know what I mean by "the risk of an accident." I'll add these two details: how rockets have been known to explode, and how astronauts, unlike tourists, are trained to handle the dangers of space flight. Now both my facts are developed by details, and my reason is better supported.

**Read the excerpt below from Luna's draft of the assignment. Then complete the activities. Use the Hints for help.**

### Luna's Draft

The IAU should have let more of its members vote. If more members had voted, they might have rejected the vague definition. Then the IAU could have made a more accurate definition everyone agrees on. It's possible that a more accurate definition would still lead to Pluto being called a dwarf planet, but at least the definition would be better and there would be less disagreement among astronomers.

**1 Ideas** One reason Luna thinks the IAU made the wrong decision is that the voting process was too flawed for making such a drastic change. Her paragraph does not state this reason. Write a sentence clearly stating the reason.

> **HINT** In the sentence stating the reason, be specific about what the IAU was voting on.

_____

_____

_____

**2 Elaboration** Luna needs more evidence to develop her reason. Suggest two facts or details Luna could add to develop her reason.

> **HINT** Review your notes to identify some facts and details that develop Luna's reason.

_____

_____

_____

_____

_____

**Turn and Talk** Take turns reading aloud your drafts. Discuss whether the reasons are clearly stated in each draft, and suggest revisions as needed.

### Write Time ✏

Use the Opinion Writing Checklist passed out by your teacher to evaluate your draft for **Ideas**, **Organization**, and **Elaboration**.

# Step 7 Revise: Second Read

**W.5.1c:** Link opinion and reasons using words, phrases, and clauses (e.g., *consequently, specifically*).

**L.5.6:** Acquire and use accurately . . . words and phrases, including those that signal contrast, addition, and other logical relationships.

**FOCUS**  Linking Words, Phrases, and Clauses

Once your ideas are organized and developed, it's time to check your word choices to make sure your letter is as clear as possible. In this step, you'll look for ways to connect important ideas and make your text flow smoothly. One way to do this is by using **linking words, phrases, and clauses.**

The bulleted words in the chart below are examples of linking words, phrases, and clauses you can use when writing an opinion text such as a letter to the editor.

| Linking Words, Phrases, and Clauses | | | |
| --- | --- | --- | --- |
| **Similarity** | **Contrast** | **Cause and Effect** | **Elaboration** |
| • likewise<br>• in the same way | • however<br>• on the other hand | • consequently<br>• one result is that | • specifically<br>• as one source says |

> **Language Handbook**  To learn more about linking words, phrases, and clauses, turn to page 228.

## 👥 Modeled Instruction

**Read the following excerpt from a draft of "Space Tourism Can Wait."**
**Then complete the activities.**

**MENTOR TEXT**  Draft

The first thing to understand is that the monetary cost of space travel is incredibly high. <u>Each trip to the Space Station costs $20 million dollars.</u> According to my research, space tourists have already made that trip eight times at a total cost of $160 million dollars. <u>As a result, millions of dollars that could have been spent helping many people instead went to a single person's idea of fun.</u> Now think of some other ways those citizens could have spent their money. They could have spent it on education or medical research.

**1** The writer wants to put the linking clause *As one source says* at the beginning of the first underlined sentence. Why is *As one source says* the correct linking clause to use?

_____

_____

_____

**2** **Draw a box** around the linking phrase in the second underlined sentence. Explain why the writer used this phrase.

_____

_____

_____

## Guided Practice

Read the following paragraph from an early draft of the Mentor Text. Then use the Hints to complete the activities that follow.

**MENTOR TEXT  Draft**

Idea 1 — It all sounds pretty exciting, right? Space tourism
Idea 2 — has problems we must consider. It is expensive. Space tourism is open to anyone with enough money, but most people can't afford it. What's worse, space — Idea 3
tourism is dangerous. A spaceship might blow up on — Idea 4
the way up, while in space, or on the way down.

**3** The writer wants to show a contrast between Idea 1 and Idea 2. Which pair of sentences below best expresses this contrast? Circle the correct answer.

> **HINT** The writer wants to show that Idea 2 is different from Idea 1.

**A** It all sounds pretty exciting, right? In the same way, space tourism has problems we must consider.

**B** It all sounds pretty exciting, right? However, space tourism has problems we must consider.

**C** It all sounds pretty exciting, right? One result is that space tourism has problems we must consider.

**D** It all sounds pretty exciting, right? Specifically, space tourism has problems we must consider.

**4** In the draft, Idea 4 is an example that elaborates on Idea 3. Which pair of sentences below best expresses this connection? Circle the correct answer.

> **HINT** The writer needs to show that Idea 4 is an example of the claim made by Idea 3.

**A** What's worse, space tourism is dangerous. In the same way, a spaceship might blow up on the way up, while in space, or on the way down.

**B** What's worse, space tourism is dangerous. On the other hand, a spaceship might blow up on the way up, while in space, or on the way down.

**C** What's worse, space tourism is dangerous. Consequently, a spaceship might blow up on the way up, while in space, or on the way down.

**D** What's worse, space tourism is dangerous. Specifically, a spaceship might blow up on the way up, while in space, or on the way down.

**Turn and Talk** Take turns reading aloud paragraphs from your letters. Point out where your partner could connect ideas more clearly with specific linking words, phrases, and clauses.

**Write Time** ✏

Use the Opinion Writing Checklist passed out by your teacher to evaluate your draft for **Language**.

# Step 8 Edit for Conventions

W.5.5: With guidance and support from peers and adults, develop and strengthen writing as needed by . . . editing.

L.5.2a: Use punctuation to separate items in a series.

**FOCUS** Punctuating a Series

The last step is to make sure that your spelling, grammar, and punctuation are correct. In this step, you'll focus on using punctuation to separate items in a series.

- A **series** is a list of three or more items. Use a **comma (,)** to separate those items.

  Space tourism is **expensive, dangerous,** and **wasteful.**

- Place a comma after each item in the series, except the last one.

  In contrast, space exploration is an **important,** a **necessary,** and a **fascinating way to spend our time and money.**

- A series can include entire phrases and clauses.

  Space exploration can **produce new technologies, discover new resources,** and **reveal the wonders of the universe.**

> **Language Handbook** To learn more about punctuating items in a series, turn to page 198.

## Modeled Instruction

**Read the following excerpt from a draft of "Space Tourism Can Wait."**
**Then complete the activities.**

**MENTOR TEXT Draft**

> Rockets used in space tourism cost a lot are dangerous and produce a lot of pollution. Some experts say that a thousand rockets a year would make as much pollution as all other air travel combined. As a result, climate changes might increase. This could melt glaciers change weather patterns and hurt our food supplies.

**1** The first sentence has a series. **Underline** each item in the series. Then **add commas** to the series in order to correct the sentence.

**2** **Draw a wavy line** under another sentence in the paragraph that needs punctuation. Rewrite that sentence on the lines below, punctuating the series correctly.

_____

_____

_____

## Guided Practice

**Read the following excerpt from an early draft of "Space Tourism Can Wait."
Then complete the activities. Use the Hints for help.**

> **MENTOR TEXT** Draft
>
> Space tourism has problems we must consider. It is expensive there is no guarantee of safety; and there are no laws about who can go to space. The only conditions seem to be that space tourists must be in good health people under the age of 14 need an adult with them and you have to have money. Is it a good thing that only the richest people can go into space? Shouldn't we wait until more people can afford it?

**3** Read this sentence from the draft of the Mentor Text:

> It is expensive there is no guarantee of safety; and there are no laws about who can go to space.

HINT First, identify the items in the series.

Which of the following correctly punctuates this sentence? Circle your answer.

**A** It is expensive there, is no guarantee, of safety; and there are no laws about who can go to space.

**B** It is expensive, there is no guarantee of safety, and there are no laws about who can go to space.

**C** It is expensive there, is no guarantee of safety, and there are no laws about who can go to space.

**D** It is expensive, there, is no guarantee, of safety, and there are no laws about who can go to space.

**4** On the lines below, rewrite the sentence with the wavy underline, using correct punctuation.

HINT Put the commas where you would naturally pause if reading the sentence aloud.

_____

_____

**Turn and Talk** Read aloud your drafts. Listen for sentences that contain series. Review each series to determine whether commas have been used correctly.

### Write Time ✏

Use the Opinion Writing Checklist passed out by your teacher to evaluate your draft for **Conventions**.

**W.5.2:** Write informative/explanatory texts to examine a topic and convey ideas and information clearly.

**W.5.7:** Conduct short research projects that use several sources to build knowledge through investigation of different aspects of a topic.

## Sharing Information

Rico's neighbor, Mrs. Swenka, wants to buy a car, but it's hard to choose among so many kinds. She knows Rico loves cars. "What kind do you think I should get, Rico?" she asks. "I just need something to get around town in."

Rico thinks for a moment and then says, "An electric car is what you need. It never needs gas. You just plug it in every night to charge it!"

Mrs. Swenka says that sounds interesting, but she wants to learn more about the car. Rico decides to do some research and write about what he finds. The tablet below shows part of the e-mail he wrote to help Mrs. Swenka decide.

When you produce informational writing, you share what you know about a topic, such as electric cars. With some research, you can share even more.

---

4:15 PM     90%

Electric cars are cleaner and cheaper to run than gas-powered cars. They produce no exhaust, so they don't pollute the air. And it costs less to charge a battery than to fill a tank with gas. Many electric cars have a fuel cost of about $500 per year, compared with at least $6,000 for gas-powered cars.

Most electric cars can travel about 80 miles on a single charge. Also, electric cars . . .

# What Is Informational Writing?

Informational writing teaches or explains a topic to readers. The writer uses facts, definitions, quotations, and examples—often from research—to develop the topic.

## KEY FEATURES | Informational Writing

- an Introduction that clearly states a topic and prepares readers to learn about the topic
- facts and details that are logically organized in paragraphs
- precise language and domain-specific vocabulary that express ideas concisely and accurately
- linking words, phrases, and clauses that connect one idea to the next
- a conclusion that restates the topic, sums up the important points, and leaves readers with something to think about

## Steps for Writing

On the following pages, you'll learn the steps for writing your own article.

| | |
|---|---|
| **Step 1** Study a Mentor Text | **Step 5** Draft Your Article |
| **Step 2** Unpack Your Assignment | **Step 6** Revise: First Read |
| **Step 3** Find Text Evidence | **Step 7** Revise: Second Read |
| **Step 4** Organize Your Evidence | **Step 8** Edit for Conventions |

The Research Path

# Step 1 Study a Mentor Text

FOCUS Read as a Writer

Before you write your article, you'll study a model. First, read to understand what it's about. Then reread to understand how it was written.

**As you reread the Mentor Text, do the numbered activities. They'll help you understand the key features of an article.**

**MENTOR TEXT: Article**

## Turn On the Power
### *by Sung-Ki Yu*

1    When you turn on a television or computer, electricity flows into it and makes it work. But where does that electricity come from? Two important sources of electricity are coal power plants and nuclear power plants. Both types of plant provide power that keeps our country running, and both have their benefits and problems.

### How It Works: Coal

2    The United States has more than 500 coal plants located all over the country. All of them are near a water source such as a river. That's because a coal plant uses water to make electricity. Here's how the process works. After coal comes to the plant, it goes into a huge furnace. As the coal burns, it creates intense heat. The heat boils water into steam. The steam is pumped into a turbine to make the turbine spin. The turbine then spins a metal shaft in a generator. This action makes electricity. The electricity then flows through transmission lines to buildings, computers, and televisions.

### How It Works: Nuclear Energy

3    There are far fewer nuclear plants than coal plants in the United States. Specifically, there are only 62 nuclear plants located in just 31 states. Just like coal plants, nuclear plants are near water because they need water to make electricity. In contrast to coal plants, nuclear plants do not burn anything. Instead, they split uranium or thorium metal into tiny pieces. When the metal splits, it releases energy that heats water into steam. Then the process is the same as for a coal plant. The steam spins a turbine within a generator, and the generator makes electricity.

**1** **Introduction** Which sentence states the writer's topic? **Draw a dashed line** under it.

**2** **Headings** Explain why the writer includes headings in his article.

_____

_____

_____

_____

_____

**3** **Linking Words, Phrases & Clauses** In paragraph 3, the writer uses three linking words and phrases to compare and contrast coal and nuclear plants. **Draw a box** around each of these words or phrases.

## Benefits

4     Both coal and nuclear plants have some benefits compared to other power sources. Coal produces power more cheaply than other sources, such as natural gas and oil. Coal plants are also reliable. They provide a steady supply of power even when there's a great need for it, such as during the hot summer months.

5     Like coal plants, nuclear plants are reliable. Unlike solar power plants, which depend on the sun, nuclear plants produce a steady supply of energy both night and day. And nuclear plants have an advantage over coal plants. They release steam, not smoke, into the air when they make electricity, and steam doesn't cause pollution.

## Problems

6     That said, coal and nuclear plants have some major problems. Coal plants spew carbon dioxide into the air, an important cause of climate change. Another problem is that coal is a nonrenewable resource. That means it can never be replaced during our lifetimes. Once we run out of coal, that's it.

7     The metals that fuel nuclear power plants are also nonrenewable resources. In addition, nuclear plants produce dangerous waste products that have to be stored carefully. Otherwise they can cause cancer and other health problems in people and animals.

## Conclusion

8     Although coal and nuclear power plants have bad side effects, people in the United States would struggle to live without them, at least for now. In 2012, coal-powered plants produced 37 percent of America's electricity, and nuclear plants produced 19 percent. Without these power sources, our TVs and computer screens might go dark.

**4** **Develop the Topic** The writer identifies three benefits and three problems with coal and nuclear power in paragraphs 4–7. **Label** the benefits **B-1**, **B-2**, and **B-3**, and the problems **P-1**, **P-2**, and **P-3**.

**5** **Domain-Specific Vocabulary** The writer uses many terms that are specific to science writing. They very clearly name or explain scientific information. In paragraph 6, **draw a box** around three of these terms.

**6** **Conclusion** In paragraph 8, why do you think the writer included the last sentence?

_____

_____

_____

_____

_____

# Step 2  Unpack Your Assignment

W.5.4: Produce clear and coherent writing in which the development and organization are appropriate to task, purpose, and audience.

Before you begin writing, read your assignment carefully to identify your task, purpose, and audience. The **purpose** of an informational article is to examine a topic and convey ideas and information clearly. As you read your assignment, look for your topic and the ideas you need to explain. Sometimes your assignment will also provide clues about how you can organize your information.

## Modeled Instruction

Sung-Ki Yu, who wrote "Turn On the Power" on pages 34–35, was given the assignment below. He read it carefully and marked up some important details.

**Read Sung-Ki's assignment. Then read the points in his Think Aloud, which tell how he identified his task, purpose, and audience.**

### SUNG-KI'S Assignment

You are a writer for a popular technology magazine. You have been assigned to write an article explaining how two important power sources, coal and nuclear energy, are used to produce electricity. Your audience likes to read about technology but is not well informed about this topic.

In your article:

- Explain how each power source works.
- Tell some benefits of each power source.
- Tell some problems with each power source.

### Think Aloud

- **Audience**  I'm writing for a technology magazine, and my readers are interested in technology but don't know much about it. This means that I'll need to clearly explain terms and ideas that they might not know.

- **Purpose**  I already know that the articles in this magazine are written to inform readers. But I see the word *explaining* in my assignment. This tells me I need to use facts and details to help my readers understand my topic.

- **Task**  I have to write an article explaining three ideas about each power source: how it works, what its benefits are, and what its problems are. Maybe I can organize my article around those three ideas, covering them one at a time. I bet I can also make my information clearer by including headings.

Now it's your turn to write an informational article. Read Your Assignment carefully. Then complete the activities, using the Hints for help.

*Hi, I'm Beau, and I'm also going to be doing this assignment.*

### Your Assignment

You are a writer for a popular technology website. You have been assigned to write an article explaining how hydroelectric plants and wind-powered turbines produce electricity. You'll be writing for people who enjoy reading about technology, but are not experts on this topic.

**To prepare to write your article, you will read the following sources:**

- Hydroelectric Power  *pages 42–43*
- Capturing the Wind  *pages 44–47*

**In your article:**

- Explain how each power source works.
- Tell some benefits of each power source.
- Tell some problems with each power source.

**1 Audience  Draw a box** around two phrases that describe your audience. What is important for you to know about them? Why is it important?

**HINT** Where will your writing be published? How much does your audience know about the topic?

_____

_____

**2 Purpose  Draw a dashed line** under the phrase that tells your purpose for writing.

**HINT** Is your writing meant to inform, entertain, or give an opinion?

**3 Task  Circle** the type of writing you will do. Then **underline** the three ideas you will develop in your writing.

**HINT** What do you need to explain or tell about each power source?

**Turn and Talk**  Discuss how the information in your assignment can help you make a plan for organizing your writing.

# The Research Path
## Writing from Sources

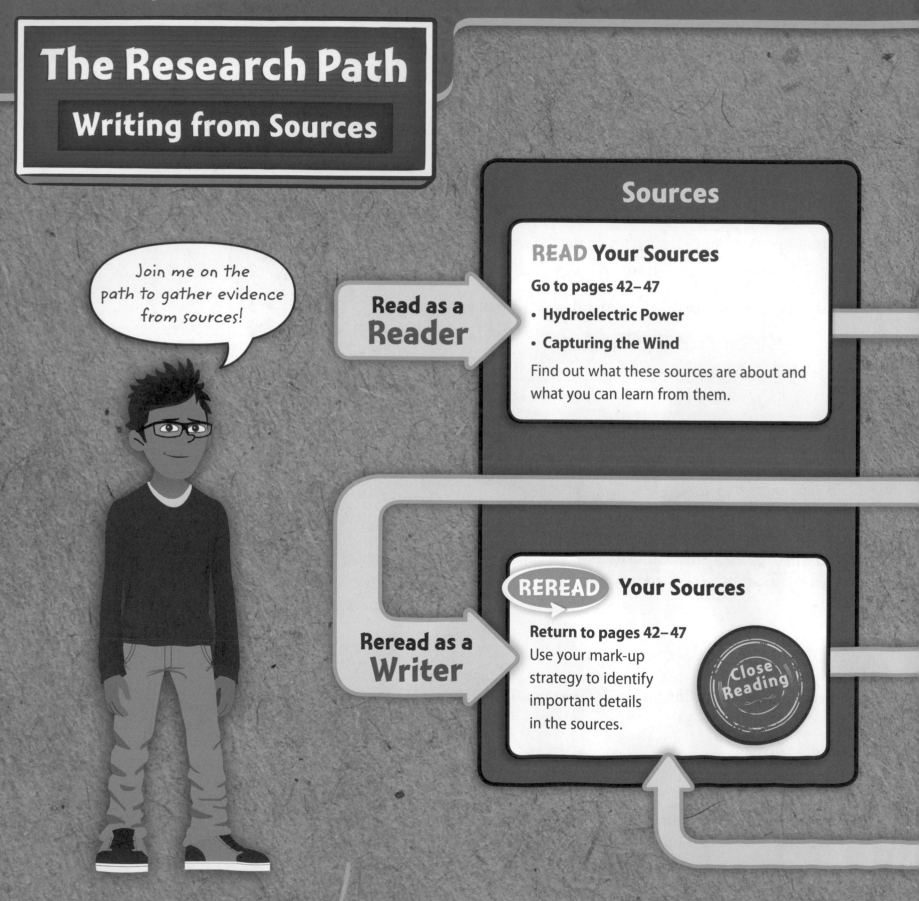

Join me on the path to gather evidence from sources!

**Sources**

**READ Your Sources**

**Go to pages 42–47**
- **Hydroelectric Power**
- **Capturing the Wind**

Find out what these sources are about and what you can learn from them.

Read as a **Reader**

Reread as a **Writer**

**REREAD Your Sources**

**Return to pages 42–47**
Use your mark-up strategy to identify important details in the sources.

Close Reading

## REVIEW Your Assignment

**Return to page 37**
Reread your task to identify the types of information you will need to include in your article.

## Text Evidence

### FIND Text Evidence

**Go to pages 40–41**
Learn how to mark important details so you can find them quickly later on.

## THINK It Through

**Go to pages 48–49**
Complete the activities to help you connect the ideas in the sources to your assignment.

### ORGANIZE Your Evidence

**Go to pages 50–51**
Use a chart to group your ideas and evidence so that you're ready to write.

### Need More Information?

### Begin Writing!
Go to pages 52–53

# Step 3 Find Text Evidence

W.5.8: . . . gather relevant information from print . . . sources. . . .

FOCUS Gather Information

You've unpacked your assignment and identified three ideas that you will develop in your article. As you reread your source texts, use the following system to label the details that will help you explain to your readers how hydroelectric plants and wind-powered turbines produce electricity.

- **How each power source works.** Underline details about the generation of hydroelectric power in the first source and wind power in the second. Mark them with a **W**, for *works*.

- **Benefits of each power source.** Underline details about the benefits, or pros, of each power source. Mark them with a **B**, for *benefit*.

- **Problems with each power source.** Underline details about the problems caused by each power source. Mark them with a **P**, for *problem*.

## Modeled Instruction

To gather information for his article, Beau underlined details and marked up the text as he read his first source, "Hydroelectric Power."

**Read the text and Beau's Think Aloud to learn about the reading and mark-up strategies he used.**

From **"Hydroelectric Power"** *page 42*

So just how do we get electricity from water? Actually, hydroelectric and coal-fired power plants produce electricity in a similar way. In both cases, a power source is used to turn a propeller-like piece called a turbine. The turbine then turns a metal   W shaft in an electric generator. The generator is the motor that produces electricity. A coal-fired power plant uses steam to turn the turbine blades. A hydroelectric plant uses falling water to turn   W the turbine. The results are the same.

**Think Aloud**

● The first sentence tells me this paragraph is about how water is used to make electricity. The next sentence says even more clearly that the paragraph will explain how hydroelectric plants produce electricity. So I'll read closely for details in the paragraph to mark with a W for *work*.

● These sentences tell how the parts of a generator work together to produce electricity. These details will help me explain how hydroelectric power works, so I'll mark them with a W.

● This sentence explains the first step in the process of generating hydroelectric power. I'll label it with a W, too.

## Guided Practice

Read the following excerpt from "Capturing the Wind" and note the underlined details. Then complete the activities, using the Hints for help.

From **"Capturing the Wind"** *page 45*

. . . Wind farms produce large quantities of clean energy. What do we  ẞ
mean by "clean" energy? Clean energy doesn't create pollution or greenhouse
gases that can contribute to climate change. In 2013, the clean energy
produced by wind power was equal to the effect of taking nearly 17 million
cars off the roads. Wind energy is also renewable, which means it can't be
used up. And it doesn't use water to create electricity.

**1** Why is the first sentence in the excerpt marked with a B? Explain your answer.

> **HINT** What is helpful about using wind farms to produce electricity?

_____

_____

_____

**2** Would you mark the second underlined sentence with a W, B, or P? Explain your answer.

> **HINT** What does the sentence explain about clean energy?

_____

_____

_____

**3** Find another benefit of wind power in the paragraph. **Underline** it and **mark** it with a B. Then explain why this detail describes a benefit.

> **HINT** What does *benefit* mean?

_____

_____

_____

**Turn and Talk** How will this system of marking the text help you organize the information in your article?

# HYDROELECTRIC POWER
## FROM THE U.S. GEOLOGICAL SURVEY

### Hydroelectric power: How it works

1 So just how do we get electricity from water? Actually, hydroelectric and coal-fired power plants produce electricity in a similar way. In both cases, a power source is used to turn a propeller-like piece called a turbine. The turbine then turns a metal shaft in an electric generator. The generator is the motor that produces electricity. A coal-fired power plant uses steam to turn the turbine blades. A hydroelectric plant uses falling water to turn the turbine. The results are the same.

### HOW A HYDROELECTRIC DAM WORKS

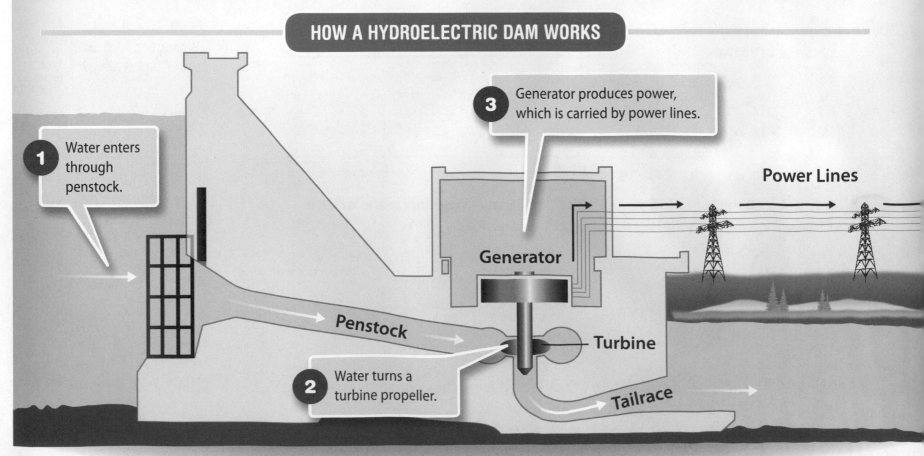

1 Water enters through penstock.

3 Generator produces power, which is carried by power lines.

**Power Lines**

Generator

Penstock

2 Water turns a turbine propeller.

Turbine

Tailrace

2     A typical hydroelectric dam is built on a big river with a large drop in elevation. The dam stores lots of water behind it in the reservoir. Near the bottom of the dam wall there is the water intake called a penstock. Gravity causes the water to fall through the penstock inside the dam. At the end of the penstock, there is a turbine propeller, which is turned by the moving water. The shaft from the turbine goes up into the generator, which produces the power.[1] Power lines connected to the generator carry electricity to your home and mine. The water continues past the propeller through the tailrace. The water then flows into the river, past the dam. By the way, it is not a good idea to be playing in the water right below a dam when water is released!

## Pumped storage: Reusing water for peak electricity demand

3     Demand for electricity is not "flat" and constant. Demand goes up and down during the day. Overnight there is less need for electricity in homes, businesses, and other facilities. For example, at 5:00 P.M. on a hot August weekend day, there may be a huge demand for electricity to run millions of air conditioners! But, 12 hours later at 5:00 A.M. . . . not so much. Hydroelectric plants are more efficient at providing for peak power demands during short periods than are fossil fuel and nuclear power plants. One way of doing that is by using "pumped storage," which uses the same water more than once.

4     Pumped storage is a method of keeping water in reserve for peak periods of power demand. Pumps move water that had already flowed through the turbines back up to a storage pool above the power plant. That happens when customer demand for energy is low, such as during the middle of the night. The water is then allowed to flow back through the turbine-generators at times when electricity demand is high.

### HYDROPOWER FAST FACTS

- It's the cheapest way to generate electricity today. Once a dam has been built and the equipment is in place, the source of energy, flowing water, is free.

- Several countries, including Canada, Brazil, New Zealand, and Switzerland, produce the majority of their electricity through hydropower.

- It's a renewable power source. Rain and snow supply the water.

- Power is readily available. A hydroelectric plant can provide electricity on demand.

- Damming rivers can destroy or disrupt animal migration patterns.

- Hydropower plants can cause low levels of oxygen in water, which is harmful to river plants and animals.

- Reservoirs, or bodies of water created by dams, can cover land needed for farming.

---

[1] For the generator to produce electricity, loops of wire must spin rapidly through force fields made by magnets.

# Capturing the Wind

*by Diane Zahler*

1    Have you ever seen an old-fashioned windmill? Windmills built long ago often look like fat wooden or stone towers. They have four **blades** or sails that turn in the wind. For more than 1,000 years, people used windmills to capture the energy of the wind. Windmills were first used to grind grain and pump water. Later, they created the energy needed to cut up lumber and process all kinds of products, from spices to paint. In the 1880s, though, engineers realized that windmills could produce electricity—and the wind turbine was born.

## How Do Wind Turbines Produce Power?

2    Wind turbines are huge windmills that usually have two or three big blades. The blades can be as long as 200 feet (60 meters)—about two-thirds the length of a football field. Wind turbines are tall—sometimes as tall as a twenty-story building—so they can catch the wind. At that height, the wind moves fast and is more reliable than the wind we feel near the ground.

### How a Wind Turbine Works

- Blades are mounted around a turning part called a **rotor**, which is connected to a part called a **shaft**.

- When the blades catch the wind, it turns them. This spins the shaft.

- The shaft is connected to a **generator**, which turns the energy from the movement of the shaft into **current electricity**, or electricity that travels through cables and wires.

Wind turbines, in fact, work exactly the opposite way fans do. A fan uses electricity to create wind. A turbine uses the wind to create electricity.

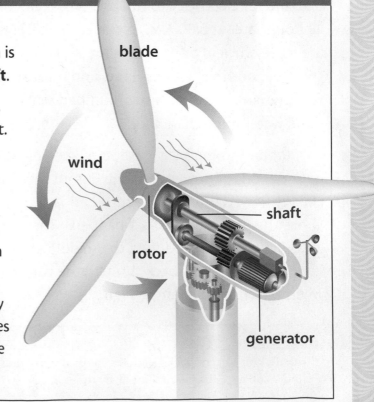

blade

wind

shaft

rotor

generator

3    Where does the wind that moves the blades come from? Curiously enough, wind power gets its start from solar power, or energy from the sun. As the sun warms the earth, different areas heat up to different temperatures. These differences cause changes in air pressure. Air moves from high-pressure areas to low-pressure areas. This movement of the air—sometimes slow, sometimes fast—is what we call wind.

## Wind Farms

4    An area of land with a group of energy-producing wind turbines is called a **wind farm**. Wind farms produce large quantities of clean energy. What do we mean by "clean" energy? Clean energy doesn't create pollution or greenhouse gases that can contribute to climate change. In 2013, the clean energy produced by wind power was equal to the effect of taking nearly 17 million cars off the roads. Wind energy is also renewable, which means it can't be used up. And it doesn't use water to create electricity. Electricity plants powered by coal or nuclear energy use water for cooling. Switching to wind power can provide water for more than a million people each year.

5    To create energy, a turbine needs winds of at least seven miles per hour. The turbine is most efficient when the winds are around thirty miles per hour. It can be difficult to find the best sites to build wind farms, though. They usually have to be located in rural places with few trees to slow the wind. Hilltops are good locations, and some wind farms in Europe are located offshore, in water. These locations make bringing the electricity to where it is most needed (usually in cities) a challenge. Power lines are required to carry the electricity, and they can be expensive.

🔑 **KEY WORDS**

**blade** a flat, wide, spinning part used to push air

**current electricity** a form of electricity that travels through cables and wires

**generator** a machine that turns energy of motion into electrical energy

**rotor** a machine part that rotates, or turns

**shaft** the long, narrow part of a machine

**watt** the unit that scientists use to measure power

**wind farm** an area of land with a group of energy-producing wind turbines

Areas with tight groupings of turbines are called *wind farms*.

A wind turbine designed to provide electricity for a single home

## Personal Wind Turbines

6    Wind turbines can also create power on a smaller scale. Some wind turbines power only a single home. (Imagine having your own windmill in the backyard or on the roof.) But not every home is right for a personal turbine. Most personal turbines are in areas far from cities or towns. A person who installs a turbine for a home must live in an area with winds of at least nine to ten miles per hour for the turbine to generate enough electricity to be useful. A personal turbine can let homeowners be energy independent or add their own electricity to the electricity they buy. This can result in low electricity costs—or even none at all. For example, one homeowner in Southern California installed a 60-foot turbine and didn't have to pay an electricity bill for the next year.

## Some Windy Problems

7    Turbines do create one kind of pollution: noise pollution. People who live close to wind farms often complain about the noise the turbines make as they turn. And there are other problems with wind turbines. Wind isn't constant: it doesn't always blow, and sometimes it blows harder than other times. Because of this, wind can't be counted on as our main source of energy.

8    Often the areas where turbines would be most efficient could be used in other ways—growing crops, for example. Some critics believe that wind turbines are ugly and ruin the landscape. And turbines have been responsible for the deaths of birds and bats that fly into them. Those who build the turbines have to consider these problems and choose sites carefully. The wind industry has been working with environmental groups to reduce the damaging effect of turbines on wildlife and the environment.

9    Once a turbine is built, the energy it produces costs very little. However, building the turbines is costly because the technology is still relatively new. That said, wind energy is a fast-growing business. By 2012, there were more than 46,000 wind turbines in the United States.

## The Future of Wind Power

10    In 2013, wind power in the United States created enough electricity to power a small city. It would take fourteen nuclear power plants or fifty-two coal plants to make that much electricity.

11    In 2009, wind power created less than two percent of the electricity used in the United States, but by 2014 that amount was greater than five percent. Some experts predict that by 2050, one-third of all the world's electricity will come from the wind.

12    Wind power has obviously come a long way since the days of grinding grain and pumping water. And while wind turbines can't be the only solution to our world's energy needs, they are one piece of a complex challenge that we all have an interest in facing up to and solving—the challenge of how we keep our society working.

## Think It Through

**Use details from both sources to complete the following activities. Your answers will help you write your article.**

**1** How does a hydroelectric plant work to produce electricity? List the steps below.

1. _____

2. _____

3. _____

4. _____

**HINT** Use the steps in both the text and the diagram to help you understand the process.

**2** How is the way that a wind turbine works similar to the way that a hydroelectric plant works? How is it different?

_____

_____

_____

_____

_____

**HINT** Use the diagrams in both sources to help you understand how each power source works.

**3** Using renewable sources of energy is a benefit of both hydroelectric power plants and wind turbines. Explain how each one uses renewable sources of energy. Then explain why this is a benefit.

_____

_____

_____

_____

**HINT** What does *renewable* mean? What energy source does each type of power plant use?

**4** Hydroelectric power and wind power are "clean" sources of energy, meaning they don't cause air pollution. However, they can still cause problems for the environment. What is one problem that each of them can cause?

HINT Look for details in both sources that you marked with a P.

**Hydroelectric Power:** _____

_____

**Wind Power:** _____

_____

**5** Based on what you read, do you think communities should keep investing in hydroelectric dams and wind turbines? Do the benefits of these power sources outweigh their problems? Explain your answer, using details from both texts.

HINT Look at the sidebars as well as the main text of the two sources.

_____

_____

_____

_____

_____

_____

_____

# Step 4 Organize Your Evidence

W.5.5: With guidance and support from peers and adults, develop and strengthen writing as needed by planning. . . .

W.5.8: . . . summarize or paraphrase information in notes . . .

**FOCUS** Plan Your Article

Now that you've gathered information from your sources, it's time to organize it. You can use the three ideas you identified in your assignment to group your details. When you write your article, each idea and related group of details will become a paragraph or section.

## 👥 Modeled Instruction

To organize his information, Beau created the chart below. Then he began adding details he underlined in his sources. He explained each detail in his own words.

**Compare the first underlined sentence from "Hydroelectric Power" with the note in Beau's chart. Then help Beau complete the next three bullets by adding details from the remaining underlined sentences.**

From **"Hydroelectric Power"** *page 43*

   A typical hydroelectric dam is built on a big river with a large drop in elevation. The dam stores lots of water behind it in the reservoir. Near the bottom of the dam wall there is the water intake called a penstock. Gravity causes the water to fall through the penstock inside the dam. At the end of the penstock, there is a turbine propeller, which is turned by the moving water. The shaft from the turbine goes up into the generator, which produces the power.

**Beau's Chart**

| Hydroelectric Plants | |
|---|---|
| How It Works | • Gravity makes water fall through the penstock.<br><br>• The water _____<br><br>_____<br><br>_____<br><br>• _____<br><br>_____<br><br>• _____<br><br>_____ |

## 👥 Guided Practice

**Read the following excerpt from "Capturing the Wind" and continue helping Beau fill in his chart by completing the activities. Use the Hints for help.**

From **"Capturing the Wind"** *page 44*

. . . Wind turbines are tall—sometimes as tall as a twenty-story building—so they can catch the wind. W At that height, the wind moves fast and is more reliable than the wind we feel near the ground.

### How a Wind Turbine Works

- Blades are mounted around a turning part called a **rotor**, which is connected to a part called a **shaft**.
- When the blades catch the wind, it turns them. This spins the shaft.
- The shaft is connected to a **generator**, which turns the energy from the movement of the shaft into **current electricity**, or electricity that travels through cables and wires.

**Beau's Chart**

| | Wind Turbines |
|---|---|
| How It Works | • Blades on the turbines catch the wind. <br> • _____ |

1️⃣ **Draw an arrow** from the underlined sentence to the matching detail in Beau's chart. Then explain why Beau put the detail in the chart.

_____

_____

> **HINT** How did Beau mark the underlined sentence?

2️⃣ Find two additional details that describe how wind power works. **Underline** them, and **mark** them with a W. Add them to the chart using your own words.

> **HINT** What happens after the blades catch the wind?

**Turn and Talk** The first section of Beau's chart lists ideas about how each power source works. Discuss what other sections the chart should have, based on your assignment.

### Write Time ✏️

In your own chart, record the evidence you marked in each source. Organize the evidence according to the idea it supports.

# Step 5 Draft Your Article

**W.5.2:** Write informative/explanatory texts to examine a topic and convey ideas and information clearly.

**W.5.2a:** Introduce a topic clearly, provide a general observation and focus, and group related information logically; include formatting (e.g., headings) . . . when useful to aiding comprehension.

**FOCUS** Write an Introduction

**Read this chart to learn more about the parts of an article. You can refer back to this information as you write your draft.**

## Parts of an Article

### INTRODUCTION

Tells what the article is about and captures readers' attention

The introduction to an article should clearly state the topic. It should also grab readers' attention and make them want to keep reading. Here are three different approaches:

- **Show the importance** of the topic in your readers' everyday lives.

- **Ask a question** to make readers curious and get them thinking about possible answers.

- **Make an observation** that will help readers know what aspect of the topic your article will focus on.

### BODY

Develops the topic with facts and details

The body of your article should include paragraphs that support and explain your topic. You should:

- **Group related information** into paragraphs.

- Include **facts, definitions, details, and examples** to develop your ideas.

- Use **headings** to tell what each major section is about.

- Use **precise language** and **domain-specific vocabulary** to present ideas accurately.

- Use **linking words, phrases, and clauses** to connect your ideas and make them easy to follow.

### CONCLUSION

Sums up what the writer wants readers to know

Conclude your article by summing up your main points. You can also use these approaches:

- **Draw a conclusion** or make a statement based on the information you presented.

- Give your readers a **final thought** about the topic.

# Draft Your INTRODUCTION

Practice writing three different approaches to an introduction. Study each example below. Then try writing in a similar way for your article.

| Show the Importance of Your Topic | |
|---|---|
| Sample Text | Imagine your life without heat, lights, television, and computers. They all depend on one thing—electricity. |
| Your Article | |

**HINT** Who is your audience? How does your topic relate to them?

| Ask a Question | |
|---|---|
| Sample Text | But what price are we willing to pay for all that electricity? |
| Your Article | |

**HINT** Consider some of the benefits and problems you learned about in your research. What do you want your audience to think about?

| Make an Observation | |
|---|---|
| Sample Text | All of the benefits we enjoy from cheap, reliable electricity come with some problems, too. |
| Your Article | |

**HINT** Think about your assignment. What ideas will your article focus on?

**Turn and Talk** Discuss how you showed your audience the importance of your topic. What are some other ideas you could try?

### Write Time

Use one or more of your ideas from this page to begin writing your introduction. Then begin writing your body paragraphs.

**W.5.2b:** Develop the topic with facts, definitions, concrete details, quotations, or other information and examples related to the topic.

FOCUS  Add Definitions and Examples

## Draft Your BODY

As you write your draft, develop your topic by providing definitions and examples to explain complex technical processes. **Definitions** help your readers understand scientific words, and **examples** illustrate how ideas play out in reality.

- A **definition** is an explanation of what a word or phrase means. Introduce a definition with a phrase such as "This means . . ." or "In other words. . . ."

- An **example** is a specific, real-world illustration of a general idea. Writers often introduce examples with phrases such as "For example . . ." or "For instance. . . ."

INTRODUCTION

BODY

CONCLUSION

## Modeled Instruction

**Read the excerpt from "Turn on the Power." Note the underlined details. Complete the activities to show how they clarify the main idea of each paragraph.**

### From MENTOR TEXT *page 35*

That said, coal and nuclear plants have some major problems. Coal plants spew carbon dioxide into the air, an important cause of climate change. Another problem is that coal is a nonrenewable resource. <u>That means it can never be replaced during our lifetimes.</u> Once we run out of coal, that's it.

The metals that fuel nuclear power plants are also nonrenewable resources. In addition, nuclear plants produce dangerous waste products that have to be stored carefully. Otherwise they can cause <u>cancer</u> and other health problems in people and animals.

**1** How does the underlined sentence in the first paragraph help readers understand the main idea of the paragraph?

_____

_____

_____

**2** **Underline** two examples of coal plants' "major problems" in the first paragraph.

**3** Read the underlined word in the second paragraph. Explain why the writer included this detail.

_____

_____

_____

## 👥 Guided Practice

Beau used his notes to write the draft below. Now he must find ways to develop his ideas with specific definitions and examples.

**Read Beau's notes and draft. Complete the activities, using the Hints for help.**

### Beau's Chart

| Hydroelectric Plants | |
|---|---|
| Benefits | • Uses a renewable resource<br>• Cheapest way to generate electricity; once plant is built, source of energy is free<br>• More efficient than fossil fuel or nuclear "for peak power demands during short periods"; can use pumped storage to keep water for later use |
| Problems | |

### Beau's Draft

Hydroelectric plants use water, a plentiful and renewable resource. Such power plants are the most inexpensive way to generate electricity. <u>They're also more efficient in many ways.</u> But they have their share of problems, too.

**4** What words could Beau define to support the first sentence in his draft?

_____

> **HINT** What science term might be unfamiliar to readers?

**5** Beau wants to include examples after the underlined sentence. On the lines below, write two sentences with examples from the source.

_____

_____

_____

> **HINT** Read the notes in Beau's chart. Which details could he use to show the efficiency of hydroelectric power plants?

💬 **Turn and Talk** Why are definitions and examples especially important to use when writing about science?

### Write Time ✏️

Finish drafting the body of your article. Then draft a conclusion using the tips from the chart on page 52 for help.

# Step 6 Revise: First Read

**W.5.4:** Produce clear and coherent writing in which the development and organization are appropriate to task, purpose, and audience.

**W.5.5:** With guidance and support from peers and adults, develop and strengthen writing as needed by . . . revising. . . .

FOCUS Ideas and Elaboration

As you revise, use your Informational Writing Checklist to check your writing. Work through the checklist, one line at a time. Reread the related parts of your article to decide whether you did your best possible work for each trait described. In this step, you will check your article for three of the traits in the categories of Ideas and Elaboration.

## Modeled Instruction

The Mentor Text writer, Sung-Ki Yu, used the same checklist to evaluate his draft.

**Read his Think Aloud to see how he checks his article.**

### MENTOR TEXT Draft

When you turn on a television or computer, electricity flows into it and makes it work. But where does that electricity come from? Two important sources of electricity are coal power plants and nuclear power plants.

**How It Works: Coal**

The United States has more than 500 coal plants located all over the country. All of them are near a water source such as a river. A river is far larger than a creek or a stream. Coal plants are near water because they use it to make electricity. Here's how the process works. After coal comes to the plant, it goes into a huge furnace. As the coal burns, it creates intense heat. The heat boils water into steam. The steam is pumped into a turbine to make the turbine spin. The turbine then makes a generator work. The electricity then flows through transmission lines to buildings, computers, and televisions everywhere.

### Think Aloud

● **Ideas** Do I state my topic clearly? My article is mainly about the good and bad points of coal and nuclear power plants. My introduction doesn't say anything about that. I'll add a sentence to the end of the paragraph to make my topic clear: "Both types of plant provide power that keeps our country running, and both have their benefits and problems."

● **Elaboration** Do I include enough facts, details, and examples to support my ideas? In the second paragraph, my main idea is "How coal plants work." I include enough details in *most* of the paragraph, but I don't say what a generator does. I'll replace "The turbine then makes a generator work" with these sentences: "The turbine then spins a metal shaft in a generator. This action makes electricity."

● **Elaboration** Are all my details clearly related to the topic? Mostly. But my second paragraph has a detail that doesn't belong: "A river is far larger than a creek or a stream." It doesn't relate to coal plants or nuclear plants, so I'll delete it.

Read the excerpt below from Beau's draft of the assignment. Then complete the activities. Use the Hints for help.

### Beau's Draft

Wouldn't it be wonderful to have sources of power that pollute little, operate cheaply, and produce electricity for millions of people? We already do: hydroelectric power plants and wind turbines.

Most of the more than 2,000 hydroelectric power plants in the United States work in the following way. At the base of a dam is an entry called a penstock. Water flows through the penstock to a turbine. The turbine spins, making a shaft in a generator rotate quickly. The spinning shaft in the generator makes electricity, which then flows through power lines.

**1 Ideas** Beau does not clearly state his topic in his first paragraph. Write a sentence that he could add to the end of the first paragraph to make his topic clear.

> **HINT** Your assignment clearly states what the article should be about.

_____

_____

**2 Elaboration** The main idea of Beau's second paragraph is how hydroelectric power plants work. Does he include enough facts, details, and examples so that his readers clearly understand this idea? Explain your answer.

> **HINT** Imagine you haven't read the sources and don't know how a dam works. What information is missing from Beau's description?

_____

_____

_____

**3 Elaboration** Are all of Beau's details related to his topic? Explain your answer.

> **HINT** Do any details seem out of place? Or do they all seem to fit?

_____

_____

💬 **Turn and Talk** Take turns reading aloud paragraphs from your drafts. Listen for whether your main ideas are supported by enough facts, details, and examples.

### Write Time ✏️

Use the Informational Writing Checklist passed out by your teacher to evaluate your draft for **Ideas**, **Organization**, and **Elaboration**.

# Step 7 Revise: Second Read

**W.5.2d:** Use precise language . . . to inform about or explain the topic.

**W.5.5:** With guidance and support from peers and adults, develop and strengthen writing as needed by . . . revising. . . .

**FOCUS** Precise Language

In this step, you'll look for ways to use **precise language**. Good writers present their ideas using words and phrases that are very specific, rather than vague, and that accurately describe what is being discussed.

The charts below show some examples of vague words and the precise words that can replace them.

| Vague | Precise |
|---|---|
| **make** | produce - "create something as part of a process" |
| **need** | demand - "a pressing requirement" |

| Vague | Precise |
|---|---|
| **good thing** | benefit - "advantage" |
| **always there** | reliable - "dependable" |

## 👥 Modeled Instruction

**Read the following excerpt from "Turn on the Power." Note how Sung-Ki Yu uses precise language to make his ideas as clear as possible. Then complete the activities.**

### From MENTOR TEXT *page 35*

   Both coal and nuclear plants have some benefits compared to other power sources. Coal <u>produces</u> power more cheaply than other sources, such as natural gas and oil. Coal plants are also reliable. They provide a steady supply of power even when there's a great need for it, such as during the hot summer months.

   Like coal plants, nuclear plants are reliable. Unlike solar power plants, which depend on the sun, nuclear plants produce a steady supply of energy both night and day. And nuclear plants have an advantage over coal plants. They release steam, not smoke, into the air when they make electricity, and steam doesn't cause pollution.

**1** In the second sentence, Sung-Ki uses the word *produces*. In an earlier draft, he used *makes*. Why did he replace this word?

_____

_____

**2** **Draw a box** around two additional examples of precise language the writer uses in the first paragraph.

**3** In the second paragraph, **cross out** a vague word the writer could replace with a precise one. Write the replacement on the line below.

_____

## Guided Practice

Read the following paragraph from an early draft of the Mentor Text. Then use the Hints to complete the activities that follow.

> **MENTOR TEXT  Draft**
>
> Coal and nuclear power plants have some bad side effects. But for now, the good things outweigh the problems. In 2012, coal-powered plants met 37 percent of America's electricity needs. Nuclear plants made 19 percent of our energy.

**4** Read this sentence from the draft:

But for now, the <u>good things</u> outweigh the problems.

Which word best replaces the underlined text in the sentence?
Circle the correct answer.

**A** supplies

**B** sources

**C** demands

**D** benefits

> **HINT** Which word is a more precise way to say "good things"?

**5** Read these sentences from the draft:

In 2012, coal-powered plants met 37 percent of America's electricity needs. Nuclear plants made 19 percent of our energy.

Rewrite the sentence on the lines below, replacing any vague words with precise words.

> **HINT** Check the chart on the opposite page for vague words that appear in these sentences.

_____

_____

_____

**Turn and Talk** Take turns reading aloud your drafts, identifying where you or your partner could use precise language to express ideas more clearly.

### Write Time

Use the Informational Writing Checklist passed out by your teacher to evaluate your draft for **Language**.

# Step 8 Edit for Conventions

W.5.5: With guidance and support from peers and adults, develop and strengthen writing as needed by . . . editing.

L.5.1e: Use correlative conjunctions (e.g., *either/or, neither/nor*).

FOCUS Correlative Conjunctions

The last step is to make sure that your spelling, grammar, and punctuation are correct. In this step, you'll focus on using **correlative conjunctions**. Conjunctions are words such as *and, but,* and *or* that join words, phrases, or parts of a sentence. Correlative conjunctions are conjunctions that are used in pairs. The chart below shows examples.

| Correlative Conjunctions | Examples |
| --- | --- |
| either . . . or | We can visit **either** a hydroelectric plant **or** a wind turbine. |
| neither . . . nor | **Neither** Beau **nor** Sung-Ki has actually seen such places. |
| both . . . and | **Both** coal **and** nuclear power plants are essential sources of power. |
| not only . . . but also | For now, our society depends **not only** on renewable energy resources **but also** on nonrenewable ones. |

**Language Handbook**  To learn more about correlative conjunctions, turn to page 196.

## Modeled Instruction

**Read the following excerpt from a draft of "Turn on the Power." Then complete the activities.**

MENTOR TEXT  Draft

Coal plants and nuclear plants share many similarities. Both coal and also nuclear power plants need sources of heat and water to produce electricity. And, both are relatively cheap and reliable after they are built. But neither coal or nuclear energy is without problems. They not only produce types of pollution but rely on nonrenewable resources to work. Still, they are an important part of modern American society.

**1** Describe how to correct the sentence with the wavy line.

_____

**2** Decide whether the underlined sentence uses correlative conjunctions correctly. If not, correct it on the line below.

_____

**3** One more sentence uses correlative conjunctions incorrectly. Find it and correct it on the lines below.

_____

_____

## Guided Practice

Read the following excerpt from an early draft of "Turn on the Power."
Then complete the activities. Use the Hints for help.

### MENTOR TEXT  Draft

Nuclear plants can use either uranium and thorium metal as a heat source. Neither uranium or thorium is common or cheap. Both are hard to find but expensive to prepare for use. Once these metals are prepared, however, nuclear energy is not only cheap or also reliable.

**4** Read this sentence from the draft:

Nuclear plants can use <u>either uranium and</u> thorium metal as a heat source.

Which of the following should replace the underlined words to make the sentence correct? Circle the correct answer.

**A**  either uranium nor

**B**  neither uranium nor

**C**  either uranium or

**D**  neither uranium and

> **HINT** The writer wants to show a choice between uranium and thorium.

**5** On the lines below, rewrite the following sentences to correct any mistakes in the use of correlative conjunctions.

Neither uranium or thorium is common or cheap. Both are hard to find but expensive to prepare for use. Once these metals are prepared, however, nuclear energy is not only cheap or also reliable.

> **HINT** Check the chart on the opposite page for correct pairings of correlative conjunctions.

_____

_____

_____

**Turn and Talk** Take turns reading aloud your drafts. Discuss whether you can connect any of your ideas by using correlative conjunctions.

### Write Time ✏

Use the Informational Writing Checklist passed out by your teacher to evaluate your draft for **Conventions**.

# Lesson 3
# Writing a Narrative: Legend

W.5.3: Write narratives to develop real or imagined experiences or events using effective technique, descriptive details, and clear event sequences.

## Sharing Stories

Tim's great-grandfather was about to have his 90th birthday. Tim had been thinking about what to give him for this special occasion, and decided to write his life story. Tim asked his mom to share details about her grandpa's life.

"Grandpa George has done a lot of great things," she said. "He flew in the Air Force. He helped build a school in my hometown. He ran his own store. And, of course, he and Grandma Louise raised four kids." Tim wrote all of this down. Then his mom said, "Grandpa George has always been my hero."

A hero! Tim imagined his great-grandfather leaping across rooftops and wearing a cape. So Tim decided to write a legend to show how important George was to his family. A **legend** is a story about a person in the past that has some truth to it. It would be George's story—made more exciting and fun to read with some new and exaggerated details. Part of what Tim wrote is shown on the tablet below.

### The Legend of George

When George was a young man, he joined the Air Force. He flew generals across the Atlantic Ocean on important missions. One night, over the ocean, a wing started to fall off. George climbed outside and fixed the wing with duct tape. Then he went back inside and had a cup of coffee.

Another time, George decided . . .

Super-George

# What Is Narrative Writing?

Narrative writing tells a story, either real or imagined. Writers use techniques, such as dialogue and description, to bring the characters and events to life.

**KEY FEATURES** | **Narrative Writing**

- a beginning that introduces the characters, the setting, and the situation—the circumstances or problem—that sets the events in motion
- a middle that shows events unfolding naturally and that describes the characters, their words and actions, and their responses to events
- dialogue that shows what the characters think and feel
- transitional words, phrases, and clauses that make the sequence of events clear
- concrete words and sensory details that help readers imagine the story
- an ending that tells how the problem is solved and brings the story to a satisfying conclusion

## Steps for Writing

On the following pages, you'll learn the steps for writing your own legend.

**The Research Path**

| | | | |
|---|---|---|---|
| **Step 1** | Study a Mentor Text | **Step 5** | Draft Your Legend |
| **Step 2** | Unpack Your Assignment | **Step 6** | Revise: First Read |
| **Step 3** | Find Text Evidence | **Step 7** | Revise: Second Read |
| **Step 4** | Organize Your Details | **Step 8** | Edit for Conventions |

# Step 1  Study a Mentor Text

FOCUS  Read as a Writer

Before you write your legend, you'll study a model. First, read to understand what it's about. Then reread to understand how it was written.

**As you reread the Mentor Text, do the numbered activities. They'll help you understand the key features of a legend.**

**MENTOR TEXT:** Legend

## The Best Gator Wrestler of 1804

*by Lily Alfarsi*

1    You've probably heard about Davy Crockett's skill at wrestling big, scaly alligators. Here's something you might not know, though. One year, another great gator wrestler challenged him for his title of "Best Gator Wrestler." Lulu Mae Hardeen, a cook from Alabama, faced Davy Crockett in the Southern States Gator Wrestling Competition of 1804, in the Great Swamp of Virginia.

2    Though still a teenager, Davy had won the contest the last four years running. Every year, three or four brave fellows came forward to challenge him, but they always lost. Sometimes they lost body parts, too!

3    Then came that hot, cloudy day in 1804. The air was as thick and heavy as a blanket, as if a storm was about to break. Still, hundreds of people turned out to watch the contest. Davy Crockett strode into the ring, faced his enormous alligator, and shouted, "Are you ready for me, gator?" The gator didn't say a word, of course, but swept its scaly tail back and forth. Faster than you could blink, Davy straddled that gator and flipped it onto its back. Then, like a cowboy roping a steer, he tied the gator's front and back legs together. The gator was defeated.

4    The next wrestler didn't do as well. He lost the tip of his finger to his gator's sharp teeth and ran away howling.

**1** **Establish a Situation**  The writer introduces Davy's problem right away. **Draw a dashed line** under the sentence that tells Davy's problem.

**2** **Sensory Details**  In paragraph 3, **underline** details that describe the setting. Why do you think the writer describes the setting this way?

_____

_____

_____

**3** **Concrete Words**  In paragraph 3, the writer shows Davy's confidence and swagger by describing his movements with very specific words and phrases. **Draw a box** around each of these words and phrases.

5    Then Lulu Mae entered the ring. She was nearly as tall as Davy. Her arms were powerful from years of kneading bread dough. She looked her big, mean gator straight in the eye and cried, "Are you ready for me, gator?" just as Davy had done. The gator gave her a big gator smile.

6    The battle began. Lulu Mae was light on her feet, dancing around the gator as it spun to snap at her. The gator got so dizzy that Lulu Mae flipped and tied it without breaking a sweat.

7    Now it was time to break the tie, and Davy was getting nervous. Could Lulu Mae Hardeen wrestle a bigger gator than he could? He and Lulu Mae stood together in the ring and shook hands.

8    "Hope you won't be a sore loser, Lulu Mae Hardeen," Davy boomed.

9    Lulu Mae waved a finger at him and tossed one of her fresh-made biscuits his way. Davy easily caught it and shoved the sweet-smelling biscuit into his pants pocket. "Hope YOU won't be a sore loser, Davy Crockett," Lulu Mae said. Then she gave him a gator-sized smile.

10    Just then, the guards led in two of the biggest gators the crowd had ever seen. Everybody clapped and cheered. Lulu Mae didn't look the least bit worried. Her gator moved on her fast. She got her hands around its snout, but it was so big she couldn't flip it. Instead, the two of them, gator and cook, just stood still. Lulu Mae kept trying to flip the beast, and the beast kept trying to escape. Each was exactly as strong as the other. Neither could move an inch.

11    Davy, on the other hand, thought fast. As his gator approached, he took the light, fluffy biscuit out of his pocket and tossed it over the gator's head. Surprised, the gator snatched at the biscuit, grabbing it and chewing it up. The biscuit was so delicious that the gator closed its eyes in pleasure. While the gator was distracted, Davy got his hands around it and flipped it, tying its legs tightly. "Cheater! Cheater!" cried the crowd.

12    The judges argued for an hour, yelling and shouting and shaking their fists. Eventually, however, they ruled that biscuits were allowed. And that is how Davy Crockett used his strength and some quick thinking to beat Lulu Mae Hardeen at gator wrestling, winning the title of "Best Gator Wrestler" of 1804.

**4** **Description** **Underline** the detail the writer uses in paragraph 5 to show Lulu Mae's strength.

**5** **Dialogue** The words that Davy and Lulu Mae say to each other in paragraphs 8 and 9 are practically the same. **Underline** the two sentences of dialogue. Then tell why you think the writer has both characters say this.

_____

_____

_____

_____

_____

**6** **Ending** The ending of a narrative should provide a satisfying solution to the problem. **Draw a dashed line** under the sentence in paragraph 12 that tells how Davy's problem is solved.

# Step 2 Unpack Your Assignment

W.5.4: Produce clear and coherent writing in which the development and organization are appropriate to task, purpose, and audience.

**FOCUS** Identify Task, Purpose, and Audience

As you have learned, the first step to planning a writing assignment is to identify your task, purpose, and audience. Unlike an opinion piece or an article, which provide information, the **purpose** of narrative writing is to entertain.

By now you are familiar with the main story elements: setting, characters, and a plot with a beginning, middle, and end. As you read your assignment, look for details about these story elements. Since you'll be writing a specific kind of narrative—a legend—look for clues about the unique story elements of a legend. Also begin thinking of creative ways to develop story details that will hold your readers' interest and keep them entertained.

## Modeled Instruction

Lily Alfarsi, who wrote "The Best Gator Wrestler of 1804" on pages 64–65, was given the assignment below. She read it carefully and marked up some important details.

**Read Lily's assignment. Then read the points in her Think Aloud, which tell how she identified her task, purpose, and audience.**

### LILY'S Assignment

You are entering a writing contest sponsored by a kids' magazine. Your assignment is to write a legend about the real-life hunter and soldier, Davy Crockett. Your legend should be set in the early 1800s in the state of Virginia. In your story, Davy will face another character in an alligator-wrestling contest. He must use strength and quick thinking to win.

**In your legend:**

- Write a beginning that establishes the setting, the main character, and a problem or challenge the character faces.
- Write a middle that shows how the main character tries to solve the problem.
- Write an ending that follows logically from what the character does in response to the problem.

### Think Aloud

- **Audience** My readers are children who read a kids' magazine. Some may be a little younger and some a little older than I am, so I'll keep my story simple but include exaggerated details that I think the older kids will enjoy.

- **Purpose** My assignment is to write a legend about Davy Crockett. A legend is a kind of narrative, or story, so I know my purpose is to entertain.

- **Task** Since a legend is a kind of story, a story map will help me organize details about the setting, characters, problem, beginning, middle, and end. This assignment gives me a lot of that information already: Davy Crockett will be a main character, and the setting will be Virginia in the early 1800s. It even tells me about my plot. There will be an aligator-wrestling contest and Davy will win. It's up to me to figure out how to make that suspenseful and exciting.

## Guided Practice

Now it's your turn to write a legend. Read Your Assignment carefully.
Then complete the activities, using the Hints for help.

*Hi, I'm Olive, and I'm also going to be doing this assignment.*

### Your Assignment

You are entering a story-writing contest at your local library. You must write a legend about a palace guard who recovers a king's stolen crown. The guard, who is known for his or her cleverness and quick thinking, has to come up with a plan for retrieving the crown from the king's enemy, who has stolen it and hidden it away in his own castle.

**To prepare to write your legend, you will read the following:**

- Legends  *pages 72–75*

**In your legend:**

- Write a beginning that establishes the setting, the main character, and the problem or situation that sets the events in motion.

- Write a middle that shows how the main character tries to solve the problem.

- Write an ending that follows logically from the character's actions.

**1 Audience**  Who do you think your audience will be? Draw a box around the word or phrase that helps you understand this. Then explain your answer.

**HINT** Where is the contest being held? Who can you infer might read the stories?

_____

_____

**2 Task  Underline** the details you must include in each part of your legend.

**HINT** What belongs in the beginning, middle, and end?

**3 Task**  Which details of your legend does your assignment provide for you?

**HINT** What is your legend about?

_____

_____

_____

**Turn and Talk**  Discuss some initial ideas for your legend. What details will make the legend entertaining to readers?

# The Research Path
## Writing from Sources

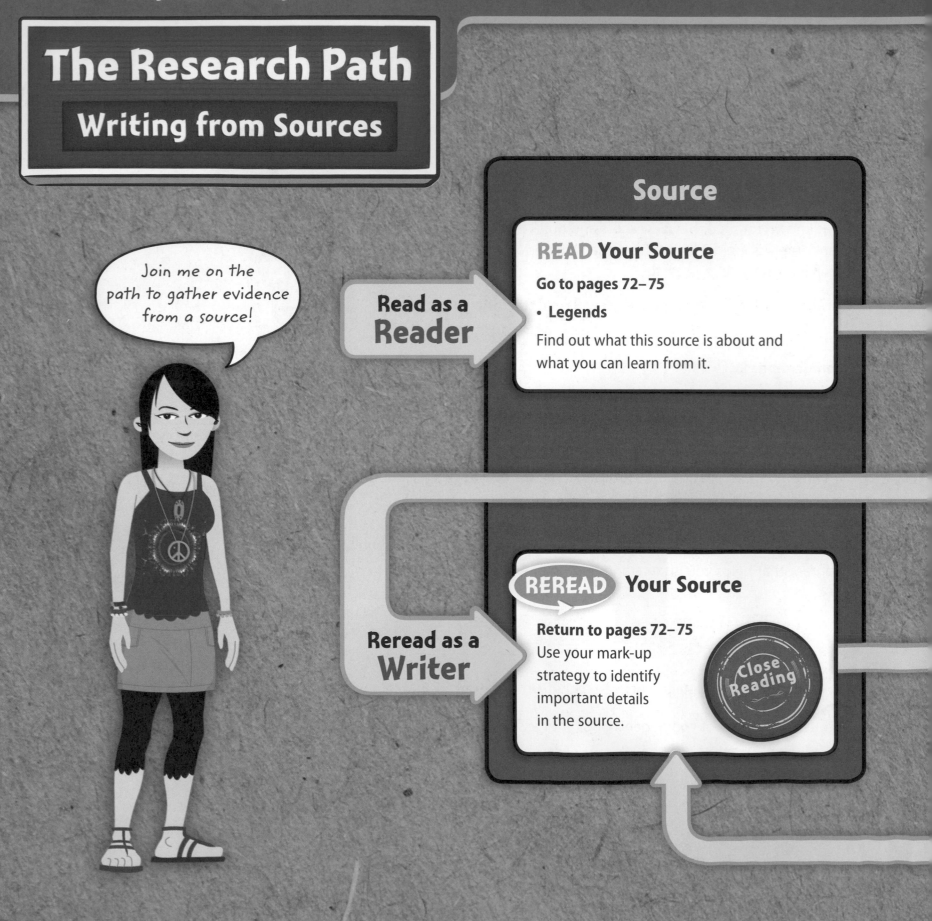

Join me on the path to gather evidence from a source!

**Read as a Reader**

### Source

### READ Your Source

**Go to pages 72–75**

- **Legends**

Find out what this source is about and what you can learn from it.

**Reread as a Writer**

**REREAD Your Source**

**Return to pages 72–75**
Use your mark-up strategy to identify important details in the source.

Close Reading

## REVIEW Your Assignment

**Return to page 67**
Reread your task to identify the types of details you will need to include in your legend.

## Text Evidence

### FIND Text Evidence

**Go to pages 70–71**
Learn how to mark important details so you can find them quickly later on.

## THINK It Through

**Go to pages 76–77**
Complete the activities to help you connect the ideas in the source to your assignment.

## ORGANIZE Your Details

**Go to pages 78–79**
Use a story map to plan each part of your legend so that you're ready to write.

**Need More Information?**

**Begin Writing!**
Go to pages 80–81

# Step 3 Find Text Evidence

W.5.8: . . . gather relevant information from print . . . sources. . . .

FOCUS Gather Information

You've unpacked your assignment and learned that you will write a specific type of narrative—a legend. You've also noted important story elements to include. Now you'll look for details in the source text describing what makes a legend different from other narratives. Specifically, look for information about the following:

- the **setting**, or where and when a legend usually takes place
- the **main character**, or hero that a legend tells about
- the **plot**, or sequence of story events, that is set in motion by a problem or challenge faced by the hero of a legend

As you reread the source text on pages 72–75, mark details that explain what is unique about the story elements of legends. Use **S** for *setting*, **C** for *character*, and **P** for *plot*. This will make it easy to review the information when you're ready to plan your legend.

## Modeled Instruction

Olive underlined details and marked up the text as she read "Legends."

**Read the text and Olive's Think Aloud to learn more about the reading and mark-up strategies she used.**

From **"Legends"** *page 72*

    **Legends** are stories that many people believe to be true, even though scholars cannot prove they are. Legends often (but not always) center on real-life heroes. Some legends also tell about real events from history. However, the facts about real-life people and events are enhanced with many fictional details. The details often are so convincing that many people accept every part of a legend as truth.

    All legends are narratives, which means they ~~ha~~ve a beginning, middle, and end, and tell a story ~~in ti~~me order.

*C*

*C+P*

*P*

### Think Aloud

- This sentence tells me that the main character in a legend is often a real-life hero, but not always. I'll underline the sentence and mark it with a C. I know from my assignment that my hero won't be a real-life person, but I will give my hero the characteristics of a real person.

- The text says that details about real people and events can be enhanced. That's cool! It means I can make up descriptions and details about my characters and events. They still have to be believable, though. I'll underline this part and mark it with both a C and a P.

- These details make me think that my legend needs a clear, sensible sequence of events. I'll need to make sure that each of my events follows naturally from earlier events, like in real life. I'll mark these details with a P.

## 👥 Guided Practice

**Read the following excerpt from "Legends." Note the underlined detail.
Then complete the activities, using the Hints for help.**

From **"Legends"** *page 73*

   . . . First, although their plots may have fantasy elements, such as magical weapons and imaginary beasts, <u>the stories happen in real places, not a fantasy S world</u>. Even if the legend is said to have happened long ago, those who hear the story today can still visit the place where it occurred. Second, legends are linked to a particular time in history as well as a particular place. . . . And third, the main characters in legends are people with extraordinary skills and virtues, not superhuman powers.

**1** Tell why the underlined detail is marked with an S.

_____

_____

_____

> **HINT** What does the S markup indicate?

> **HINT** Which sentence gives a detail about when legends take place?

**2** Setting is not only about where a story takes place. **Underline** another important detail about the setting of a legend, and **mark** it with an S.

**3** Find a detail about characters in legends. **Underline** the detail and **mark** it with a C. Explain how this detail adds to what you already know about the main characters in legends.

> **HINT** Think about how you will develop your main character.

_____

_____

_____

_____

💬 **Turn and Talk** Discuss what is meant by "fantasy elements." Make a list of some that might be appropriate to the plot of your legend. Use your imagination, but keep in mind that legends are set in a real time and place in history.

# Encyclopedia for Kids

LOG IN    ABOUT    HELP         SEARCH  [                    ] 🔍

# Legends

**Contents ▼**

Introduction

Special Features of Legends

Legend, Myth, or Fairy Tale?

The Legendary Problems of Real and Fictional Heroes

  King Arthur

  Queen Amina of Zaria

  John Henry

  William Tell

  Hua Mulan

## Introduction

1    **Legends** are stories that many people believe to be true, even though scholars cannot prove they are. Legends often (but not always) center on real-life heroes. Some legends also tell about real events from history. However, the facts about real-life people and events are enhanced with many fictional details. The details often are so convincing that many people accept every part of a legend as truth.

2    All legends are narratives, which means they have a beginning, middle, and end, and tell a story in time order. Like all stories, legends usually introduce the characters, setting, and problem in the first few paragraphs. The middle paragraphs tell about the events of the story and how the characters think, feel, and react to what happens. The last few paragraphs—the end—tell how the characters solve their problem and bring the story to a satisfying conclusion.

LOG IN   ABOUT   HELP          SEARCH

# Special Features of Legends

3      In addition to sharing the features of a
narrative, legends share three special features.
First, although their plots may have fantasy
elements, such as magical weapons and
imaginary beasts, the stories happen in real
places, not a fantasy world. Even if the legend
is said to have happened long ago, those who
hear the story today can still visit the place
where it occurred. Second, legends are linked
to a particular time in history as well as a
particular place. For example, the legend of
King Arthur is usually set in England during
the fifth century. And third, the main characters
in legends are people with extraordinary skills
and virtues, not superhuman powers. In the
King Arthur legend, Arthur and his knights are the main characters. They are
extraordinary people, but they are just people. They struggle, not just with
enemies, but also with personal flaws such as pride, anger, or recklessness.

Nobody knows for sure what
King Arthur looked like, but
many drawings of him are based
on descriptions from literature.

4      Despite setting events in specific times and places, legends also express
timeless themes—ones that people can learn from today. These include the
values of fighting injustice, defending a nation, and overcoming personal
weaknesses.

# Legend, Myth, or Fairy Tale?

5      People often find it hard to tell the difference between legends, myths, and
fairy tales. Most experts place these stories into a larger category called
**folklore**. However, the three types of stories differ in important ways.

6      **Fairy tales** are clearly make-believe. They take place in fantasy worlds and
describe impossible characters and events. By contrast, the heroes in legends
often do amazing things, but they use real human skills, not magical ones.

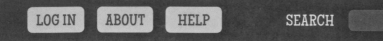

LOG IN    ABOUT    HELP        SEARCH

7    **Myths** center on supernatural beings such as gods and goddesses. Myths often try to explain something, such as the creation of the world or the causes of natural events like floods, earthquakes, or eclipses. In contrast, legends tell about the deeds of human heroes dealing with human problems.

# The Legendary Problems of Real and Fictional Heroes

8    Cultures around the world tell tales of legendary heroes. As noted above, some legendary heroes are based on real people. Others are purely fictional. But they all use their extraordinary personal qualities to overcome obstacles.

## King Arthur

9    King Arthur may have been a real-life human hero. Some experts believe his legend is based on a fifth-century British ruler who defended his kingdom from invaders and helped build a nation. The stories include fantasy elements such as a magician and an enchanted sword. Their main focus, however, is on the human heroes and their struggles, both against others and with their own flaws.

## Queen Amina of Zaria

10    The legend of Queen Amina of Zaria is based on a real 16th-century African warrior-princess. One story claims that, when Amina was young, her grandmother found her holding a dagger exactly as a warrior would. This foretold her future as a skilled and brave warrior who would build a nation in what is now the country of Nigeria.

| LOG IN | ABOUT | HELP | | SEARCH | | 🔍 |

### John Henry

11  John Henry is the subject of a famous American legend about an incredibly strong man who died while competing with a steam-powered machine to carve out a railroad tunnel. People still argue about whether John Henry was a real person, but many believe he was.

### William Tell

12  The Swiss hero William Tell probably did not exist. According to legend, he was a brave patriot who helped free Switzerland from a harsh ruler in the 14th century. Most people know him as the man who was forced to shoot an apple off his son's head with a crossbow.

### Hua Mulan

13  Hua Mulan is another character who probably never existed. She is the heroine of an ancient Chinese poem that later grew into a legend. Hua Mulan disguised herself as a boy so she could be a warrior in order to honor her family and serve her country. Her story became the subject of a 1998 cartoon movie.

14      Whether new or ancient, all legends share timeless themes that reflect our values, beliefs, and ideals. A legendary hero is, at heart, a lot like us: someone who battles the odds and strives to do the right thing.

W.5.9b: Apply *grade 5 Reading standards* to informational texts.

## Think It Through

**Use details from "Legends" to complete the following activities. Your responses will help you write your legend.**

**1** List the three special features of legends identified in the source text.

1. _____

2. _____

3. _____

_____

> **HINT** The headings in the source text will help you find this information.

**2** Your assignment provided you with details about your legend: The main character is a clever palace guard who serves a king. The king's crown has been stolen and hidden in another castle. Explain how these details, along with what you've learned about the features of legends, help you determine your setting. Then describe your setting.

_____

_____

_____

_____

> **HINT** What stories with kings and castles have you read? Where and when did they take place?

**3** Although set in a real time and place, legends often include elements of fantasy. Versions of the King Arthur legend, for example, include an enchanted sword and a wizard named Merlin. What fantasy elements will you include in your legend?

_____

_____

_____

_____

> **HINT** What person, creature, or object might affect the story events—for good or bad?

**4** Review the heroes on pages 74–75 of "Legends." Some were real people, others probably never lived. But they all had extraordinary skills and virtues. Describe some of the qualities these legendary heroes shared.

**HINT** What heroic acts made these people famous?

_____

_____

_____

_____

**5** Despite extraordinary skills and virtues, the heroes in legends are a lot like everyday people in many ways. Based on the source text, explain how heroes are like regular people. Then describe the qualities of the hero in your legend. What makes him or her regular and ordinary? extraordinary?

**HINT** Reread the features of legends described in paragraph 3 on page 73.

_____

_____

_____

_____

_____

**6** What will your hero do to be honored (remembered) in a legend? Write your ideas below.

**HINT** Think about the themes common to legends. What motivates your main character to do heroic things?

_____

_____

_____

_____

# Step 4 Organize Your Details

W.5.5: With guidance and support from peers and adults, develop and srrengthen writing as needed by planning. . . .

FOCUS Plan Your Story

Now that you've begun to develop your legend's characters and setting, it's time to plan the details of your plot. Remember that narratives, including legends, are organized in the following way:

- The **beginning** introduces the main character, the setting, and the problem or situation that sets the events in motion.

- The **middle** tells the story events in order. It shows the characters thinking, feeling, and reacting to events.

- The **end** wraps up the story in a convincing way. It tells how the problem is solved.

Make a story map like the one below to help you develop the elements of your legend. You can use the story map as you write.

## Modeled Instruction

**To plan her legend, Lily Alfarsi created the story map below. Study the map and read Lily's Think Aloud. Find out how she developed the plot of her legend.**

### Lily's Story Map

**Setting:** A hot, humid day in the Great Swamp of Virginia in 1804

**Main Character:** Davy Crockett, famous hunter and soldier; strong and smart

**Problem:** Davy needs to protect his reputation as the "Best Gator Wrestler."

**Beginning:** Davy Crockett competes against Lulu Mae Hardeen in the Southern States Gator Wrestling Competition.

**Middle:** Lulu Mae, a cook, is just as good at wrestling gators as Davy. She tosses Davy a biscuit to show that she is a good sport.

**End:** Lulu Mae can't flip her gator. Davy tricks his by throwing it Lulu Mae's biscuit. He wins the contest.

### Think Aloud

- My assignment said to write a legend about Davy Crockett, a real person. He's strong and smart, but I can make up other details about him. So I'll make him a bit of a showoff, and I'll make his toughest opponent a woman who is just as strong as he is. That will be an interesting challenge!

- I know the middle of a story needs to keep readers excited, so I'll make Lulu Mae a really good wrestler, and I'll create suspense by sending the contest to a tie. The two characters will boast in a good-natured way to one another.

- Davy will win the contest. He's the hero, after all. But it will be because he uses his quick thinking and wits, not just his strength, to beat Lulu Mae.

Read the excerpt from "Legends" and help Olive fill in part of her story map by completing the activities. Use the Hints for help.

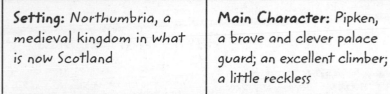

From **"Legends"** *page 73*

   . . . And third, the main characters in legends are people with <u>extraordinary skills and virtues</u>, not superhuman powers. In the King Arthur legend, Arthur and his knights are the main characters. They are extraordinary people, but they are just people. They struggle, not just with enemies, but also with <u>personal flaws</u> such as pride, anger, or recklessness.

   Despite setting events in specific times and places, legends also express timeless themes—ones that people can learn from today. These include the values of <u>fighting injustice</u>, defending a nation, and overcoming personal weaknesses.

**Olive's Story Map**

| **Setting:** Northumbria, a medieval kingdom in what is now Scotland | **Main Character:** Pipken, a brave and clever palace guard; an excellent climber; a little reckless |
|---|---|

**Problem:** Pipken must recover the king's stolen crown.

**Beginning:** The king's enemy has hidden the crown in the tower of his castle.

**Middle:** _____

_____

_____

**1** Which parts of Olive's setting are typical of legends? Explain your answer.

_____

_____

> **HINT** Review your source for the special features of legends.

**2** Which details in Olive's story map are examples of the underlined features in the excerpt? **Underline** these details in Olive's map. Then **draw an arrow** connecting each detail in the excerpt to its related detail in the map.

> **HINT** Which parts of the story map describe Pipken and his problem?

**3** Think about Pipken's plan to get back the crown. Give Olive some ideas by adding details about the plan to her map.

> **HINT** How will Pipken's cleverness and climbing ability help him find and retrieve the crown?

**Turn and Talk** Discuss your ideas for the beginning, middle, and end of your legend. What personal quality, object, or animal helps your hero find and bring back the crown? What events might add suspense, excitement, or humor?

**Write Time** ✏

Plan the parts of your legend by completing your own story map.

# Step 5 Draft Your Legend

**W.5.3:** Write narratives to develop real or imagined experiences or events using effective technique, descriptive details, and clear event sequences.

**W.5.3a:** Orient the reader by establishing a situation and introducing a narrator and/or characters; organize an event sequence that unfolds naturally.

**FOCUS** Write a Beginning

Review the main parts of a legend. Refer back to this information as you write your draft. Be sure to include each of the main parts.

## Parts of a Legend

### BEGINNING

Introduces the main character, setting, and problem

A good beginning does more than just introduce the story elements. You must also grab your readers' attention. There are several ways to do this:

- Start with **dialogue** that makes your readers wonder what's going to happen next.
- Place your main character in a **scene** that conveys information about the characters, setting, or problem.
- Describe the main character's situation in **exaggerated language** to add drama or humor.

### MIDDLE

Shows the character trying to solve his or her problem

A good middle shows the sequence of events unfolding naturally. As you develop your events:

- Include the main character's **thoughts**, **feelings**, and **actions** in response to events.
- Establish a clear event sequence, using **transitional words**, **phrases**, **and clauses**.
- Use **concrete language** and **sensory details** to help readers experience events and bring them to life.

### END

Wraps up the story and tells how the character solves the problem

A good ending leaves your readers feeling satisfied. It should:

- Tell how the character **solves the problem** and show what happens as a result.
- **Follow logically** from the earlier events.

# Draft Your BEGINNING

Practice different techniques for opening your legend. Study each sample. Then try writing a similar opening for your legend.

**BEGINNING**

MIDDLE

END

| | Start with Dialogue |
|---|---|
| Sample Text | "For four years running, I've won the Southern States Gator Wrestling Competition," declared Davy Crockett. "And I'm a-goin' to win it again!" |
| Your Legend | _____ _____ _____ |

**HINT** Let your dialogue prepare readers for the action to come.

| | Place Your Main Character in a Scene |
|---|---|
| Sample Text | Davy Crockett strode around the ring, feeling energized by the crowd's cheers. Now all he needed was a gator. |
| Your Legend | _____ _____ _____ |

**HINT** Think about where the character is when the problem arises.

| | Describe the Situation in Exaggerated Language |
|---|---|
| Sample Text | By now you've probably heard about Davy Crockett's skill at wrestling slimy, scaly alligators more than twice his size. To him, it was as common as getting dressed. |
| Your Legend | _____ _____ _____ |

**HINT** Use concrete words and exaggerated details to make the situation seem fun or dramatic.

**Turn and Talk** Discuss your opening sentences and make suggestions for how to improve them using the techniques above.

## Write Time

Draft the beginning of your legend, using ideas from this page. Then begin drafting the middle part of your legend.

**W.5.3b:** Use narrative techniques, such as dialogue, description, and pacing, to develop experiences and events or show the responses of characters to situations.

FOCUS Use Dialogue, Description, and Pacing

## Draft Your MIDDLE

As you develop your plot, make sure your events unfold naturally by carefully using these narrative techniques:

- **Dialogue**, the conversation between two or more characters in a story, shows the characters' thoughts and feelings. Make the dialogue sound the way people talk to each other in real life. This will make your story more interesting.

- **Description** helps readers share in what the characters experience.

- **Pacing**, the speed at which story events unfold, keeps the action flowing and the reader engaged. Vary the pacing. A fast pace can create excitement, while a slow pace may work better when describing a setting, for example.

## Modeled Instruction

**Read the excerpt from "The Best Gator Wrestler of 1804." Note the underlined details, and complete the activities to understand how the writer develops the plot.**

### From MENTOR TEXT *page 65*

The battle began. Lulu Mae was light on her feet, dancing around the gator as it spun to snap at her. The gator got so dizzy that Lulu Mae flipped and tied it without breaking a sweat.

Now it was time to break the tie, and Davy was getting nervous. Could Lulu Mae Hardeen wrestle a bigger gator than he could? He and Lulu Mae stood together in the ring and shook hands.

"Hope you won't be a sore loser, Lulu Mae Hardeen," Davy boomed.

**1** How does the writer use pacing in the first underlined sentence to keep readers interested?

_____

_____

**2** Why do you think the writer chose the words *dizzy* and *without breaking a sweat* to describe this scene?

_____

_____

**3** What does this dialogue tell you about Davy's response to the story's events so far?

_____

_____

Olive used her story map to write the draft below. Now she wants to add more dialogue, description, and pacing to develop her story events.

**Read Olive's notes and draft. Complete the activities, using the Hints for help.**

### Olive's Story Map

**Middle:** Pipken scales the tower, using special rope, carrying dog in backpack
- dog sniffs king's nightcap to find scent
- Pipken and dog creep through tower and find crown
- Pipken reaches for crown, but it disappears
- dog not fooled by invisible crown and grabs it
- Pipken and dog escape out window as guards appear

### Olive's Draft

Pipken crawled around the next curve of the tower on his hands and knees, following Pup's white tail. Ahead was a table. And there on the table was the crown! Pipken reached for it, but it disappeared. Pup wasn't fooled, though. Some magic had made the crown invisible, but it was still there. Pup grabbed it in his mouth. Then Pipken threw his rope around a vine, picked up Pup and the crown, and climbed out the window.

**4** How can Olive use dialogue at the beginning of the paragraph to show what Pipken is thinking and feeling?

_____

_____

> **HINT** Remember that Pipken is not all alone. He can talk to his dog.

**5** Which of Olive's notes could she use to make the crown scene come alive?

_____

_____

> **HINT** What's most surprising about the scene with the crown?

> **HINT** Concrete action words can help quicken the pace and add suspense to a narrative.

**6** How could Olive improve the pacing at the end of the paragraph to create more suspense?

_____

_____

💬 **Turn and Talk** Read your draft aloud. Identify places where dialogue and description would quicken the pace and add excitement to your legend.

### Write Time ✏️

Finish drafting the body of your legend. Then draft the ending, using the tips from the chart on page 80 for help.

# Step 6 Revise: First Read

**W.5.4:** Produce clear and coherent writing in which the development and organization are appropriate to task, purpose, and audience.

**W.5.5:** With guidance and support from peers and adults, develop and strengthen writing as needed by . . . revising. . . .

**FOCUS** Organization and Elaboration

As you revise, use your Narrative Writing Checklist to check your writing. Work through the checklist, one line at a time. Reread the related parts of your legend to decide whether you did your best possible work for each trait described. In this step, you will practice checking your legend for three of the traits in the categories of Organization and Elaboration.

## Modeled Instruction

The Mentor Text writer, Lily Alfarsi, used the same checklist to evaluate her draft.

**Read her Think Aloud to see how she checks her legend.**

### MENTOR TEXT Draft

Just then, the guards led in two huge gators. Lulu Mae's gator moved on her fast. She got her hands around its snout, but it was so big she couldn't flip it. Instead, the two of them, gator and cook, just stood still. Lulu Mae kept trying to flip the beast, and the beast kept trying to escape. Each was exactly as strong as the other. Neither could move an inch. Davy, on the other hand, moved fast. As his gator approached, he took the light, fluffy biscuit out of his pocket and tossed it over the gator's head. Surprised, the gator snatched at the biscuit, grabbing it and chewing it up. While the gator was distracted, Davy got his hands around it and flipped it, tying it tightly. "Cheater! Cheater!" cried the crowd.

The judges chatted for an hour about whether biscuits were allowed. At the end, they decided that it was fair to use biscuits. They ruled Davy Crockett the winner. The fight was over.

### Think Aloud

● **Elaboration** Do I include enough concrete words and sensory details to help readers visualize events and characters? I have some, such as *huge, snout, light, fluffy,* and *snatched,* but I should have more. I'll add more details about how big the gators are and how the crowd and Lulu Mae react to that. That'll help readers understand that this is no ordinary contest.

● **Organization** Do I use paragraphs to separate events or parts of the story? I separate my ending from Lulu Mae's and Davy's fights with the gators. That's good. A story's ending should stand out from the middle part. But I cram both Lulu Mae's and Davy's fights into one paragraph. I should have two paragraphs here: one for Lulu Mae's fight, one for Davy's.

● **Organization** Does my ending follow logically from earlier events and make the story feel finished? Not really. Would the judges just "chat" for an hour after such a controversial contest? No way! I'll change it so the judges argue about the biscuits. My ending should be more satisfying, too. I'll remind the readers that Davy is a hero because he uses brains, as well as strength, to win the contest.

## Guided Practice

**Read the excerpt below from Olive's draft of the assignment. Then complete the activities. Use the Hints for help.**

### Olive's Draft

As Pipken and Pup fled the enemy castle with the crown, they heard a dreadful barking and howling. Armed guards and a pack of huge hounds were chasing them! And as fast as they ran, the hounds kept getting closer. Finally, Pipken reached a forest and scrambled up a tall tree with Pup and the crown. The dogs stopped at the bottom of the tree. Pipken regretted his reckless plan and decided he might as well give up and throw the crown to the ground.

**1** **Elaboration**  Olive creates drama and excitement by having dogs pursue Pipken out of the castle. Does she include enough details to help the reader visualize the chase? What other details could she add?

> **HINT** How could Olive make the chase seem longer and more tiring? How can she make the dogs scarier?

_____

_____

_____

**2** **Organization**  How many events does Olive include in her draft? Are her events broken correctly into paragraphs? Explain your answer.

> **HINT** If the story were a movie, how many different scenes would this part have?

_____

_____

_____

**3** **Organization**  Olive's draft trails off with Pipken ready to give up the crown to the king's enemy. Is this a satisfying and logical ending? Explain your answer.

> **HINT** Would a hero really not try to escape the dogs?

_____

_____

_____

**Turn and Talk**  Take turns reading your endings. Evaluate whether your endings are satisfying and, if necessary, suggest how they might be improved.

### Write Time ✏

Use the Narrative Writing Checklist passed out by your teacher to evaluate your draft for **Ideas**, **Organization**, and **Elaboration**.

# Step 7 Revise: Second Read

W.5.3c: Use a variety of transitional words, phrases, and clauses to manage the sequence of events.

W.5.5: With guidance and support from peers and adults, develop and strengthen writing as needed by . . . revising. . . .

**FOCUS** Transitional Words, Phrases, and Clauses

Once your details are developed and organized, it's time to make sure your events are arranged in a clear and logical sequence. In this step, you'll look for places to use **transitional words, phrases, and clauses** to make the sequence of events clear.

- You can describe whether events happen **before** or **after** each other.

  <u>At first</u>, Pipken couldn't believe his eyes. But <u>then</u> he saw Pup grab something solid.

- You can also describe whether two or more events happen **at the same time**.

  <u>As</u> Pipken raced away, Pup whimpered. <u>Meanwhile</u>, the hounds were gaining.

The chart below shows other examples of transitional words, phrases, and clauses you can use to show the sequence of events in a narrative text.

| Before | After | At the Same Time |
|---|---|---|
| • earlier on<br>• before that happened | • after that happened<br>• an instant later | • during that time<br>• while that was happening |

## Modeled Instruction

**Read the following excerpt from "The Best Gator Wrestler of 1804." Note how Lily Alfarsi used transitional words, phrases, and clauses to manage the sequence of events. Then complete the activities.**

**From MENTOR TEXT** *page 65*

Davy, on the other hand, thought fast. <u>As his gator approached</u>, he took the light, fluffy biscuit out of his pocket and tossed it over the gator's head. Surprised, the gator snatched at the biscuit, grabbing it and chewing it up. The biscuit was so delicious that the gator closed its eyes in pleasure. While the gator was distracted, Davy got his hands around it and flipped it, tying it tightly. "Cheater! Cheater!" cried the crowd.

The judges argued for an hour, yelling and shouting and shaking their fists. Eventually, however, they ruled that biscuits were allowed.

**1** The writer used the underlined clause to show two events happening at the same time. What are those two events?

_____

_____

**2** **Underline** another phrase that signals two events happening at the same time. Describe those two events.

_____

_____

**3** **Draw a box** around the word that tells when the judges are finished arguing.

Read the following paragraph from an early draft of the Mentor Text. Then use the Hints to complete the activities that follow.

**MENTOR TEXT** Draft

Davy Crockett strode into the ring, and the crowd watched eagerly. The wranglers brought in an enormous alligator. Crockett faced his gator and shouted, "Are you ready for me?" The gator, not saying a word, lunged at Crockett. Davy straddled the gator and flipped it onto its back. Then, like a cowboy roping a steer, he tied the gator's front and back legs together.

**4** Read the following sentences from the draft:

Davy Crockett strode into the ring, and the crowd watched eagerly. The wranglers brought in an enormous alligator.

**HINT** Which answer choice shows Davy and the wranglers moving at the same time?

The writer wants to show the wranglers' action happening when Davy enters the ring. How should the writer revise the second sentence? Circle the correct answer.

**A** In a few moments, the wranglers brought in an enormous alligator.

**B** Before that happened, the wranglers brought in an enormous alligator.

**C** Meanwhile, the wranglers brought in an enormous alligator.

**D** Eventually, the wranglers brought in an enormous alligator.

**5** Read the following sentences from the draft:

The gator, not saying a word, lunged at Crockett. Davy straddled the gator and flipped it onto its back.

**HINT** Which answer choice shows Davy's actions happening as quickly as possible?

The writer wants to show Davy's actions happening just after the gator charges. Which is the best revision for the writer to make? Circle the correct answer.

**A** After a few moments, Davy straddled the gator and flipped it onto its back.

**B** Before that happened, Davy straddled the gator and flipped it onto its back.

**C** Within a minute, Davy straddled the gator and flipped it onto its back.

**D** An instant later, Davy straddled the gator and flipped it onto its back.

**Turn and Talk** Evaluate your middle paragraphs for transitional words, phrases, and clauses. Discuss how using the right transitions not only clarifies the sequence of events but can also make a scene more vivid.

**Write Time**

Use the Narrative Writing Checklist passed out by your teacher to evaluate your draft for **Language**.

# Step 8 Edit for Conventions

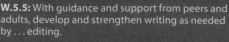

W.5.5: With guidance and support from peers and adults, develop and strengthen writing as needed by . . . editing.

L.5.1c: Use verb tense to convey various times, sequences, states, and conditions.

**FOCUS** Verb Tenses

The last step is to make sure that your spelling, grammar, and punctuation are correct. In this step, you'll focus on using verb tenses.

**Verb tenses** tell readers when something happens, in the past, present, or future. Narratives are usually set in the past, but you can use different forms of the past tense to describe exactly when events occurred. Two forms of the past tense are **simple** and **progressive**. The following chart explains how each tense works.

|  | **Simple Past Tense** | **Past Progressive Tense** |
|---|---|---|
| **Shows . . .** | a complete action from beginning to end | an action that was in progress, but had not yet ended, when the narrator observed it |
| **Example** | Pedro climbed the tree. | Pedro was climbing the tree. |

Past progressive verbs use the *-ing* ending and a helping verb such as *was* or *were*.

> **Language Handbook**  To learn more about simple and progressive verb tenses, turn to page 192.

## Modeled Instruction

**Read the following excerpt from a draft of "The Best Gator Wrestler of 1804." Then complete the activities.**

**MENTOR TEXT**  **Draft**

The guards led in two enormous gators. Everybody clapped and cheered. Lulu Mae didn't look worried. Her gator moved on her fast. She was wrapping her hands around its snout, but it was too big to flip. Instead, the two of them stood still. Lulu Mae kept trying to flip the beast, and the beast kept trying to escape. Each was as strong as the other. Neither could move an inch.

**1** The writer wants to show that the applause continued throughout the scene. How should the second sentence be revised to use the past progressive tense?

_____

_____

**2** Read the second underlined sentence. On the lines below, rewrite the sentence using the simple past tense.

_____

_____

## Guided Practice

**Read the following excerpt from an early draft of "The Best Gator Wrestler of 1804." Then complete the activities. Use the Hints for help.**

**MENTOR TEXT** Draft

> Davy moved fast. His gator got closer, so he took the biscuit out of his pocket and tossed it over its head. The surprised gator was snatching at the biscuit, grabbing it, and chewing it up. The biscuit was so delicious that the gator closed its eyes. A moment later, Davy had gotten his hands around that gator and flipped it, tying it tightly. "Cheater! Cheater!" cried the crowd.

**3** Read this sentence from the draft:

> His gator got closer, so he took the biscuit out of his pocket and tossed it over its head.

Which word or words should replace the underlined verb to show that Davy acted while the gator advanced? Circle the correct answer.

**A** has gotten

**B** is getting

**C** was getting

**D** gets

**HINT** The writer wants to show the gator in the middle of its approach when Davy tosses the biscuit.

**4** Read this sentence from the draft:

> The surprised gator was snatching at the biscuit, grabbing it, and chewing it up.

On the lines below, rewrite the sentence with the correct verb tense for the underlined words.

**HINT** Each of these actions takes place briefly, one after another.

_____

_____

**Turn and Talk** Take turns reading aloud sentences from your drafts. Listen for verb tenses that don't sound right, or that leave you confused about when something happened. Together figure out how to correct them.

### Write Time ✏️

Use the Narrative Writing Checklist passed out by your teacher to evaluate your draft for **Conventions**.

# Writing to Analyze Literature: Essay

**W.5.9:** Draw evidence from literary . . . texts to support analysis, reflection, and research.

**W.5.2:** Write informative/explanatory texts to examine a topic and convey ideas and information clearly.

## Sharing Ideas About Literature

Ella has just read an amazing short story called "Life Is But a Dream." In the story, the main character, Luka, finds herself caught between two different worlds: one a beautiful and happy place called Hope City, and the other a dark and sinister land. Luka can't be certain which world is real, and which is just a dream.

Fascinated by the story, Ella can't wait to chat about it with her friend Maya. Ella and Maya enjoy reading the same stories, and Ella always loves to hear Maya's point of view. Some of their chat is shown below.

As the girls discuss different parts of the story, they are analyzing it. Thinking carefully about the details in the story helps them understand it better.

 **Ella**
● online

 Oh my gosh, I loved it! I couldn't put it down! I think I know which one is the real world, but what do you think?

Hope City is too good to be true. It has to be a dream. But the dark world is too terrible to be true—I think! I can't decide.

 I think Hope City is real because that's where Luka's best friend is. The theme of friendship shows up a lot in the book.

Maybe, but I'm not so sure. In the dark world, Luka has to face challenges and learn to be a hero. In Hope City, everything is too easy. That's not how things are in real life.

# What Is Literary Analysis?

In a literary analysis, a writer examines and expresses his or her point of view about an element of a literary text, such as character, plot, setting, or theme. A literary analysis is based on the writer's interpretation, or understanding, of the text.

| KEY FEATURES | **Literary Analysis Essay**

- an introduction that names the literary text and prepares readers to examine a particular aspect of the text
- clearly stated ideas presented in a logical order and supported by direct quotations and examples from the text
- linking words, phrases, and clauses that connect one idea to the next
- a conclusion that sums up the writer's analysis and offers a thoughtful idea about the text

## Steps for Writing

On the following pages, you'll learn the steps for writing your own literary analysis essay.

**The Research Path**

| | |
|---|---|
| **Step 1** Study a Mentor Text | **Step 5** Draft Your Essay |
| **Step 2** Unpack Your Assignment | **Step 6** Revise: First Read |
| **Step 3** Find Text Evidence | **Step 7** Revise: Second Read |
| **Step 4** Organize Your Evidence | **Step 8** Edit for Conventions |

# Step 1 Study a Mentor Text

Before you write your essay, you'll study a model. First, read to understand what it's about. Then reread to understand how it was written.

**As you reread the Mentor Text, do the numbered activities. They'll help you understand the key features of a literary analysis essay.**

---

**MENTOR TEXT: Essay**

## The Wolf's Side of the Story
### by Philip Yee

1    Have you ever noticed that a story can change depending on who's telling it? In *The True Story of the Three Little Pigs!*, author John Scieszka presents the famous children's story as told by the Big Bad Wolf. The wolf's version of the story shows just how big a difference a narrator's point of view can make.

2    The original story of "The Three Little Pigs" is told by a narrator who describes the wolf as a "big, bad" animal. The pigs, on the other hand, are portrayed as innocent victims of a wolf who wants to blow their houses down and eat them for lunch. But in *The True Story of the Three Little Pigs!*, it's the wolf's turn to tell the story, and he clearly states his point of view. For instance, right at the beginning, he says, "I don't know how this whole Big Bad Wolf thing got started, but it's all wrong." This sentence sets up the rest of the story, in which we see all of the events from the wolf's point of view.

3    The wolf sees himself as kind and good, and behaving the way a wolf should behave. He also shares information only he would have, and that readers didn't get in the original story. For example, when we first meet him, the wolf is making a birthday cake for his "dear old granny." This detail makes the wolf seem thoughtful and caring—not big or bad at all!

**1 Introduction** How does the question in paragraph 1 help the writer introduce the topic of his essay?

_____

_____

_____

**2 Evidence** In paragraph 2, the writer provides a quotation from the story that clearly shows the wolf's point of view. **Underline** this quotation.

**3 Linking Words, Phrases & Clauses** In paragraph 3, what phrase does the writer use to connect an idea with evidence from the text? **Draw a box** around the phrase.

4      The wolf's point of view also changes the story when he describes his three encounters with the pigs. According to the wolf, he just had a bad cold that day. When he came to the house made of straw to borrow sugar for granny's cake, he sneezed so hard that he blew the house down by accident. "That's when my nose started to itch," he says. "I felt a sneeze coming on. Well I huffed. And I snuffed. And I sneezed a great sneeze. And you know what? The whole darn straw house fell down."

5      The wolf has the same explanation for what happened when he visited the house made of sticks. He describes the events of this encounter as an accident, which again shows that he didn't mean to hurt anybody. He probably would have said the same thing about the third house, but it was too strong to be taken down by a sneeze. The wolf explains that he only tried to break down the door because the pig inside had made a rude comment about his granny. "Now I'm usually a calm fellow," the wolf says. "But when somebody talks about my granny like that, I go a little crazy." From the wolf's point of view, he had every right to try to break down the door.

6      In his version of events, the wolf presents himself as completely innocent. He never changes his belief that the original story is "all wrong" and that his reputation is unfairly earned. For example, he explains the fact that he ate the first two pigs by saying, "Hey, it's not my fault that wolves eat cute little animals like bunnies and sheep and pigs. That's just the way we are." This shows that the wolf doesn't believe it was wrong to eat the first two pigs. He was just doing what wolves do.

7      *The True Story of the Three Little Pigs!* shows that a narrator's point of view can greatly affect the way events and descriptions of other characters are presented. It's hard not to like the wolf in this story when he tells it himself, but all you have to do is read the original to get a very different picture of what happened. This is an important reminder that there are two sides to every story.

**4 Evidence** In paragraph 4, what type of evidence does the writer use to support his idea that the wolf's point of view changes the original story?

_____

_____

_____

**5 Analysis** In paragraphs 5 and 6, **draw a box** around each phrase the writer uses to signal that he is explaining his thinking about these parts of the story.

**6 Conclusion** The writer sums up his analysis in the conclusion. **Draw a dashed line** beneath the sentence where he does this.

W.5.4: Produce clear and coherent writing in which the development and organization are appropriate to task, purpose, and audience.

# Step 2  Unpack Your Assignment

Before you begin writing your essay, read your assignment closely. Look for information that will help you plan your writing.

- Figure out the specific parts of the **task**, or assignment. What are you being asked to do? What information will you need to include in your writing?

- Identify your **purpose** for writing. What do you want your audience to know or understand after reading?

- In most literary analysis assignments, your **audience** is not stated. For these types of assignments, assume that your audience is your teacher and classmates.

## 👥 Modeled Instruction

Philip Yee, who wrote "The Wolf's Side of the Story" on pages 92–93, was given the assignment below. He read it carefully and marked up some important details.

**Read Philip's assignment. Then read the points in his Think Aloud, which tell how he identified his task, purpose, and audience.**

### PHILIP'S Assignment

In the book *The True Story of the Three Little Pigs!*, the narrator is the wolf who eats two of the three little pigs. As the story begins, the wolf states that he doesn't deserve his reputation as the "Big Bad Wolf." Write an essay in which you examine how this point of view influences the way the wolf describes the events in the story.

**In your essay:**

- Explain why the narrator believes he doesn't deserve his reputation as the Big Bad Wolf.

- Tell how the narrator's point of view influences the way he describes his three encounters with the pigs.

- Explain whether the narrator's point of view changes by the end of the story, and if so, how.

### Think Aloud

- **Audience**  My assignment doesn't name my audience. However, I'm writing this for a class in school, so I know that my audience is my teacher and my classmates. They are familiar with my topic.

- **Purpose**  This sentence tells me I'll be examining the wolf's point of view. My purpose is to clearly explain to my audience how the wolf's point of view influences the way the events in the story are described.

- **Task**  My task is to write an essay. The three bullet points tell me the three ideas I need to cover in my essay. I think I will organize these ideas in the same order that they're listed here. I also notice the directions *explain why, tell how,* and *explain whether.* These words signal that I need to give details from the story to support each idea and then tell why I think each detail supports the idea.

Now it's your turn to write a literary analysis essay. Read Your Assignment carefully. Then complete the activities, using the Hints for help.

*Hi, I'm Sweet T, and I'm also going to be doing this assignment.*

## Your Assignment ✏️

In the story "The Girl with the Rainbow Skin," the narrator is a Teleote, a type of advanced human. As the story begins, she believes herself to be better than normal humans. Read the story, and write an essay examining how the narrator's point of view influences the way she reacts to the humans she meets.

**In your essay:**

- Explain how the Teleote views herself.

- Tell how the Teleote's point of view influences the way she describes her three encounters with humans.

- Explain whether the Teleote's point of view changes by the end of the story and, if so, how.

**1** **Purpose** **Draw a dashed line** beneath the details that tell what you will examine in your writing. Then describe in your own words your purpose for writing.

_____

_____

**HINT** What will your topic be?

**2** **Task** **Circle** the type of writing you will do. Then **underline** the three ideas you need to cover in your writing.

**HINT** Each bulleted item begins with a verb. What information follows each verb?

**3** **Task** The third bulleted item contains two steps. Describe both steps below.

_____

_____

_____

**HINT** The words *whether* and *if* give a clue that two options are possible for this part of the task.

**Turn and Talk** Compare your assignment to Philip's assignment. Will the structure of your essay be similar to Philip's essay?

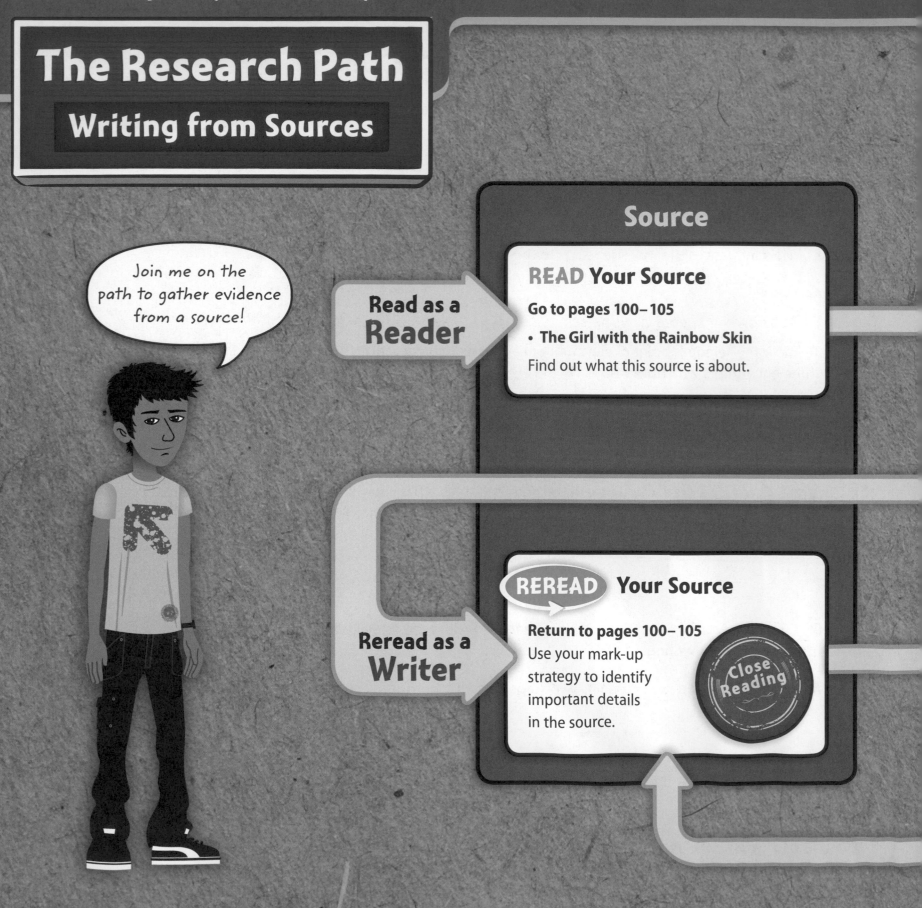

# The Research Path
## Writing from Sources

Join me on the path to gather evidence from a source!

**Read as a Reader**

## Source

### READ Your Source

**Go to pages 100–105**

- **The Girl with the Rainbow Skin**

Find out what this source is about.

**Reread as a Writer**

**REREAD** **Your Source**

**Return to pages 100–105**
Use your mark-up strategy to identify important details in the source.

Close Reading

## REVIEW Your Assignment

**Return to page 95**
Reread your task to identify the types of details you will need to include in your essay.

## FIND Text Evidence

**Go to pages 98–99**
Learn how to mark important details so you can find them quickly later on.

### Text Evidence

## THINK It Through

**Go to pages 106–107**
Complete the activities to help you connect the details in the source to your assignment.

## ORGANIZE Your Evidence

**Go to pages 108–109**
Use a chart to group your ideas, quotations, and analysis so that you're ready to write.

### Need More Information?

### Begin Writing!
**Go to pages 110–111**

W.5.8: . . . gather relevant information from print . . . sources. . . .

# Step 3 Find Text Evidence

You've unpacked your assignment, and you know that your essay will focus on the Teleote's point of view throughout the story. Now you will reread the story closely and mark the evidence you will use to develop the following ideas in your essay:

- How does the Teleote view herself? Mark these details with an **S**, for *self*.

- How does the Teleote's point of view influence the way she describes her three encounters with humans? Mark details for Encounter 1 with **E-1**, details for Encounter 2 with **E-2**, and details for Encounter 3 with **E-3**.

- Does the Teleote's point of view change by the end of the story? Mark any details showing a change with a **C**, for *change*.

## Modeled Instruction

To gather evidence for his essay, Sweet T underlined details and marked up the text as he read "The Girl with the Rainbow Skin."

**Read the text and Sweet T's Think Aloud to learn more about the reading and mark-up strategies he used.**

From **"The Girl with the Rainbow Skin"** *page 101*

E-1  Before I can tell him my name, the girl moves closer and sees the glowing colors on my face and arms.

"What are you?" she asks in a harsh whisper. "Look at her, Keahi. There's something wrong with her."

S  How dare an Organic say that about me? She is the one with the dry, dull skin that does nothing but cover her body like an envelope. Suddenly, I feel an emotion I have never experienced before, one that makes me hot and tense inside.

### Think Aloud

- This is part of the first encounter that the Teleote has with the humans. I'll mark the section with E-1 so I can keep track of everything that happens during this encounter, paying close attention to how the Teleote describes the events.

- This is interesting. When the human girl says that something is wrong with the Teleote, the Teleote thinks, "How dare an Organic say that about me?" She then criticizes the human's "dry, dull skin." The Teleote is shocked that a human would dare to insult her, and in turn she insults the human. This detail is evidence that the Teleote views herself as better than humans. I'll underline these sentences and mark them with an S.

## Guided Practice

**Read the following excerpt from "The Girl with the Rainbow Skin." Then complete the activities, using the Hints for help.**

> From **"The Girl with the Rainbow Skin"** *page 103*
>
> My first encounter with Organics hasn't gone very well, yet I can't stop thinking about them. Sometimes I touch the mucus on my skin and remember how the girl called it slime. We Teleotes think of ourselves as the most perfect humans ever created, designed to adapt to any condition on Earth. But it seems Organics think of us differently—as freaks, as the girl called Rachel said.
>
> Yet the boy did not seem to find me repulsive, and I find myself wanting to talk to him again, to see what more I can learn about Organics. One night I leave the compound and track him to the place where he lives, following the electrical signals he gives off.

**1** The first sentence contains the words *first encounter*. Should this sentence be marked with an E-1? Explain your answer.

_____

_____

**HINT** Does the first sentence give details of an interaction between the Teleote and the humans?

**2** Which idea does the underlined sentence support? Use the markup instructions on page 98 to **mark** the sentence. Explain your answer.

_____

_____

**HINT** Here, the Teleote refers to herself as a member of a group.

**3** **Underline** a detail that shows the Teleote's point of view changing. **Mark** the detail, and explain your answer.

_____

_____

**HINT** At first, the Teleote feels angry toward the humans.

**Turn and Talk** Discuss how this system of marking the text will prepare you to write your essay.

**Lesson 4** Writing to Analyze Literature: Essay

# THE GIRL WITH THE RAINBOW SKIN

**by Valentina Sanchez**

1   My skin shines as I step into the Hawaiian sunlight. Blue, green, and pink shimmer under the layer of shiny mucus that covers every inch of my bare arms and legs. I look like I am painted with liquid pearls, like an enchanted creature from a fairy tale. My people, the Teleotes, are taught to be modest, but I must be honest: my skin is pretty amazing.

And it performs beautifully, too, just as it has been made to do. I dive into the warm depths of the Pacific and swim happily beneath the waves for hours, never coming up for air. I don't need gill slits in my neck to breathe. My body can get oxygen from the water and absorb it directly through my skin into my bloodstream.

As I glide through the water, I sense something in the distance. There's a vibration about a mile away, and electricity as well. The electricity prickles behind my nose, and I turn and start swimming toward it.

A great dark shadow appears out of the sea and glides along beside me: a shark. I am not afraid—why would I be? I have shark as well as human genes. This shark and I, we are like cousins, swimming side by side, and I know it will not harm me.

5    Soon I notice two boards floating on the surface above me, and I poke my head above water, my lungs taking over from my skin so that I can continue to breathe.

That's when I discover something I have never seen before, except on a computer screen: two Organic children, a girl and a boy, about the same size as I am. Before I can greet them, one of them starts screaming.

"Shark! Hurry, get back to shore!" the girl shrieks, her voice shrill with fear.

The girl starts turning her board toward the black sand of the beach, keeping one eye on the shark all the while.

"Grab onto my board!" the boy shouts back at me. "There's a shark behind you!"

10    "I know," I say calmly, and I nod at the shark, which turns and swims away.

The girl stops paddling and asks, in a low voice, "How did you do that?"

"And where did you come from?" the boy asks. "One minute Rachel and I are alone on our surfboards, and the next minute you pop out of nowhere."

"I was just swimming," I answer.

He paddles closer and holds out a hand. "I'm Keahi. Who are you?"

15    Before I can tell him my name, the girl moves closer and sees the glowing colors on my face and arms.

"What are you?" she asks in a harsh whisper. "Look at her, Keahi. There's something wrong with her."

How dare an Organic say that about me? She is the one with the dry, dull skin that does nothing but cover her body like an envelope. Suddenly, I feel an emotion I have never experienced before, one that makes me hot and tense inside.

The boy stares at my damp, glistening skin for several seconds before asking, "Is that mucus?"

"Ewww, she's covered with slime!" the girl cries.

20 "Be quiet, Rachel," the boy says, then looks at me and adds, "You're a Teleote, aren't you? Your skin—the scientists made it like that, right?"

"You mean she's a Synthetic?" the girl says.

"That word is rude," the boy snaps. "The correct term is Teleote."

I think to myself, *The boy is smarter than I would have expected, even with his limited brain.*

"Yes, I am a Teleote," I say. "The name comes from the Greek word for *perfect*."

25 "And you probably think that people who weren't cooked up in a lab are imperfect," the girl says. "Well, I think you're a freak. Let's get out of here, Keahi."

The two of them paddle off, but Keahi looks over his shoulder at me as they move toward the shore.

My first encounter with Organics hasn't gone very well, yet I can't stop thinking about them. Sometimes I touch the mucus on my skin and remember how the girl called it slime. We Teleotes think of ourselves as the most perfect humans ever created, designed to adapt to any condition on Earth. But it seems Organics think of us differently—as freaks, as the girl called Rachel said.

Yet the boy did not seem to find me repulsive, and I find myself wanting to talk to him again, to see what more I can learn about Organics. One night I leave the compound and track him to the place where he lives, following the electrical signals he gives off.

His house and yard are filled with too much noise, too much light, and far too many people. Some are eating, and some are thrashing their bodies very fast while loud sounds play, which makes me wonder if they're having seizures.

30   I am about to leave when Keahi spots me and calls, "How'd you know where I live?"

"I figured it out," I say. "Teleotes have nine senses, not just five, so we can gather information easily. Besides, you are making so much noise that even an Organic could find you. Is this what you call a 'riot'?"

Keahi laughs and says, "This is what we call a party!"

"What is it for?" I can't figure out why anyone would want a horde of people eating all their food, messing up their home, and making so much noise that it's impossible to think.

"It's for fun!" he says.

35   "Fun is something one enjoys doing, right? I can understand that idea," I say. "I have fun swimming in the ocean, but—this party—I don't think it looks like fun."

"You don't like dancing and talking and eating delicious food?" Keahi asks. "I won't ask my parents to invite you to our next party, then!" Now Keahi looks embarrassed and says, "I guess since you weren't born like we were, you don't know about parents."

"I don't have two adult people who are responsible for raising me, if that's what you mean," I say. "I live in a scientific compound with the Elders. They're much older than I am, but they aren't my parents."

"So these Elders—do they watch over you?" Keahi asks.

"Why would I need anyone to do that?" I reply. "A Teleote's brain is fully formed from the day we first become aware. No matter how new we are, we already possess all the knowledge we need to make wise decisions."

40      An adult female voice calls out Keahi's name. He says, "I'm sorry, but I have to go. I do have parents, and they don't think I'm wise enough to make my own decisions, so they're going to tell me I'm up past my bedtime. I hope I'll see you again—maybe surfing sometime."

I do not answer. I am starting to believe that Teleotes and Organics shouldn't mix. We're just too different.

After that, I leave the compound each day and dive in the ocean, swimming in the waters near the black sand beach, where I first saw the Organics. Sometimes I see Keahi and Rachel there, but I stay underwater and don't approach them.

One day I swim past a coral reef into the open ocean. Even that far from shore, I suddenly sense a strong vibration, as if something is churning the water, and then an electric buzz starts behind my nose. And I sense something more alarming: blood in the water, the blood of an Organic.

I swim toward the black sand beach, moving as fast as my powerful muscles will allow. Not far from shore, I pass a shark and gesture angrily at it. It swims quickly out to sea.

45    Then I spot them: Rachel is clinging to her board, one arm bleeding, and Keahi floats beside her, panic on his face.

Organics are so easily hurt, and so hard to fix. But I know how to help this one.

I wipe some mucus off my skin and gently rub it into the ragged shark bite. This slime, as Rachel once called it, is filled with healing substances, and within moments, the bleeding stops and the wound begins to close.

"You'll be fine now," I say quietly.

"Thank you," Rachel says, holding out her hand to me.

50    I grasp it and smile, and then I start to swim away.

"Wait!" Keahi calls. "I've been out here looking for you every day. I thought maybe we could surf together, but now—I think we'll stay out of the water for a little while."

"I understand," I say, "But I'll keep an eye on the sharks for you and make sure they don't cause you any more trouble."

Keahi says, "Hey—any chance you'd like to give parties another chance? Our neighbors are having one tonight. Rachel and I are both invited, and they said we could bring a friend."

I think for a moment: the loud sounds, the bright lights, the people moving so fast. . . .

55    But my new friends will be there.

I say, "Yes, that sounds like fun."

W.5.9a: Apply *grade 5 Reading standards* to literature.

## Think It Through

Use details from "The Girl with the Rainbow Skin" to complete the following activities. Your answers will help you write your essay.

**1** Explain how the Teleote views herself and others like her. Support your answer with at least two details from the story.

> **HINT** Look for details in the story you marked with an S.

_____

_____

_____

_____

**2** How does the Teleote's point of view influence the way she describes her encounters with the Organics, or humans? Complete the chart below.

> **HINT** Compare the way you as a human would describe the event with the narrator's description.

| Narrator's Description | What makes the description unusual? |
|---|---|
| "I know," I say calmly, and I nod at the shark, which turns and swims away. | |
| His house and yard are filled with too much noise, too much light, and far too many people. Some are eating, and some are thrashing their bodies very fast while loud sounds play, which makes me wonder if they're having seizures. | |
| Organics are so easily hurt, and so hard to fix. But I know how to help this one. I wipe some mucus off my skin and gently rub it into the ragged shark bite. | |

**3** What does the Teleote think about humans the first two times she meets them? Provide two quotations, along with analysis that explains what each quotation shows about her point of view.

**HINT** Look at the details you marked as E-1 and E-2.

Quotation (1st encounter): _____

_____

Analysis: _____

_____

_____

Quotation (2nd encounter): _____

_____

Analysis: _____

_____

_____

**4** How does the Teleote feel about the humans at the end of the story? Provide a quotation to support your answer.

**HINT** Look for details you marked with both E-3 and C.

_____

_____

_____

_____

# Step 4 Organize Your Evidence

W.5.5: With guidance and support from peers and adults, develop and strengthen writing as needed by planning . . .

W.5.8: . . . summarize or paraphrase information in notes. . . .

FOCUS Plan Your Essay

Now it's time to organize your evidence so you're ready to write. Remember that you used a different code to mark evidence for each idea you will develop in your essay. As a result, you should organize each set of evidence according to the idea it supports.

In a literary analysis essay, you must support your ideas with quotations and analysis that makes your thinking clear and convincing. By grouping quotations and analysis together in a chart, along with the idea they support, you gather the necessary information for each paragraph you will write in your essay.

## Modeled Instruction

To organize his notes about the Teleote's three encounters with the humans, Sweet T created the chart below.

**Notice the organization of Sweet T's chart. Then read the passage and add the missing analysis to the chart.**

From **"The Girl with the Rainbow Skin"** *page 101*

E-1 Before I can tell him my name, the girl moves closer and sees the glowing colors on my face and arms.

"What are you?" she asks in a harsh whisper. "Look at her, Keahi. There's something wrong with her."

S    How dare an Organic say that about me? She is the one with the dry, dull skin that does nothing but cover her body like an envelope. Suddenly, I feel an emotion I have never experienced before, one that makes me hot and tense inside.

**Sweet T's Chart**

| Encounter 1: Meeting in the Ocean ||
|---|---|
| Quotation | Analysis of Quotation |
| "How dare an Organic say that about me? She is the one with the dry, dull skin that does nothing but cover her body like an envelope." | The Teleote feels defensive. She insults the human's skin. This shows that she thinks her skin is better than the human's. |
| "I feel an emotion I have never experienced before, one that makes me hot and tense inside." |  |

**Read the following excerpt from "The Girl with the Rainbow Skin," and continue helping Sweet T fill in his chart by completing the activities. Use the Hints for help.**

From **"The Girl with the Rainbow Skin"** *page 103*

E-2   . . . "Besides, you are making so much noise that even an Organic could find you. <u>Is this what you call a 'riot'?</u>"

Keahi laughs and says, "This is what we call a party!"

"What is it for?" I can't figure out why anyone would want a horde of people eating all their food, messing up their home, and making so much noise that it's impossible to think.

"It's for fun!" he says.

"Fun is something one enjoys doing, right? I can understand that idea," I say. "I have fun swimming in the ocean, but—this party—I don't think it looks like fun."

**Sweet T's Chart**

| Encounter 2: The Party ||
|---|---|
| **Quotation** | **Analysis of Quotation** |
| "Is this what you call a 'riot'?" _____ _____ _____ _____ | |
| _____ _____ _____ | The Teleote thinks she does not have much in common with the humans. She does not consider what they do for enjoyment to be fun. |

**1** Read the quotation in Sweet T's chart. How does this quotation support the idea that the Teleote's point of view influences the way she describes this encounter with the humans? Write your answer beside the quotation in the Analysis of Quotation section of the chart.

> **HINT** A *riot* is a noisy, violent public disorder. Why does the Teleote use this word?

**2** Read the analysis in Sweet T's chart. Then read the excerpt to identify which quotation the analysis explains. Write the quotation in the chart beside the analysis.

> **HINT** A quotation can be words with or without quotation marks.

💬 **Turn and Talk** Discuss which quotations from the Teleote's third encounter with the humans you might use in your essay. Share your analysis for each quotation.

**Write Time** ✏️

In your own chart, record the evidence you marked in the story. Organize the evidence according to the idea it supports.

# Step 5 Draft Your Essay

W.5.2: Write informative/explanatory texts to examine a topic and convey ideas and information clearly.

W.5.2a: Introduce a topic clearly, provide a general observation and focus, and group related information logically. . . .

**FOCUS** Write an Introduction

Review the main parts of a literary analysis essay. Then refer back to this information as you write your draft to be sure you include each part.

## Parts of a Literary Analysis Essay

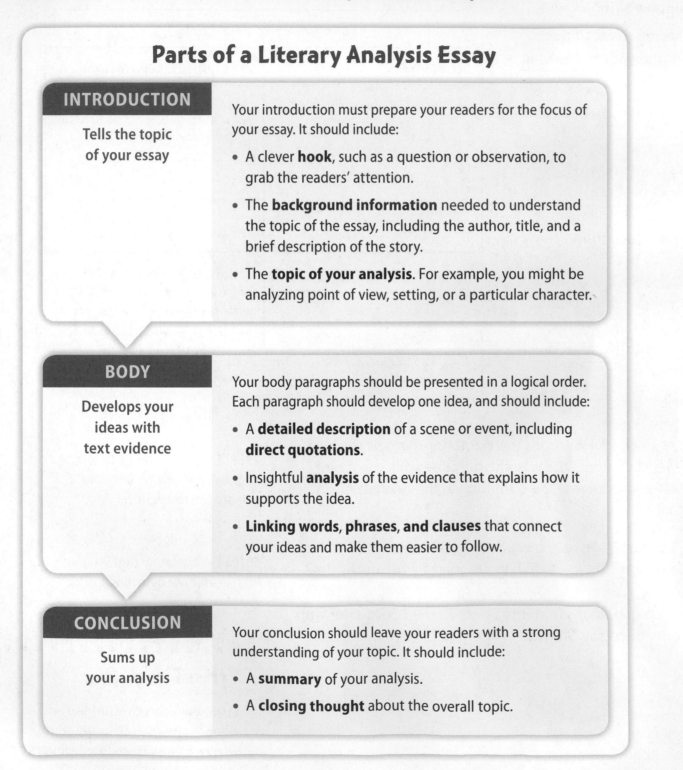

**INTRODUCTION**

Tells the topic of your essay

Your introduction must prepare your readers for the focus of your essay. It should include:

- A clever **hook**, such as a question or observation, to grab the readers' attention.
- The **background information** needed to understand the topic of the essay, including the author, title, and a brief description of the story.
- The **topic of your analysis**. For example, you might be analyzing point of view, setting, or a particular character.

**BODY**

Develops your ideas with text evidence

Your body paragraphs should be presented in a logical order. Each paragraph should develop one idea, and should include:

- A **detailed description** of a scene or event, including **direct quotations**.
- Insightful **analysis** of the evidence that explains how it supports the idea.
- **Linking words**, **phrases**, **and clauses** that connect your ideas and make them easier to follow.

**CONCLUSION**

Sums up your analysis

Your conclusion should leave your readers with a strong understanding of your topic. It should include:

- A **summary** of your analysis.
- A **closing thought** about the overall topic.

# Draft Your INTRODUCTION

Practice writing the parts of your introduction. Study each example from the Mentor Text. Then try to do something similar in your own essay.

**INTRODUCTION**

BODY

CONCLUSION

## Hook Your Reader

| Mentor Text | Have you ever noticed that a story can change depending on who's telling it? |
|---|---|
| Your Essay | _____<br>_____<br>_____ |

> **HINT** What is interesting or unusual about the story? How might you turn this into a question?

## Provide Background Information

| Mentor Text | In *The True Story of the Three Little Pigs!*, author John Scieszka presents the famous children's story as told by the Big Bad Wolf. |
|---|---|
| Your Essay | _____<br>_____<br>_____ |

> **HINT** Name the title and author, and provide a brief description of the story.

## State Your Topic

| Mentor Text | The wolf's version of the story shows just how big a difference a narrator's point of view can make. |
|---|---|
| Your Essay | _____<br>_____<br>_____ |

> **HINT** Reread your assignment. What will you examine in your essay?

**Turn and Talk** Discuss how you can make your first sentence interesting. Practice different ways of beginning your essay and decide which you like best.

## Write Time ✏️

Use your ideas from this page to begin drafting your introduction. Then begin drafting your body paragraphs.

W.5.2b: Develop the topic with facts, definitions, concrete details, quotations, or other information and examples related to the topic.

FOCUS  Add Quotations

## Draft Your BODY

Remember that as you write your essay, you will develop your ideas with examples that include quotations. A **quotation** is one or more words copied directly from the story and set between quotation marks. Here are two ways to use quotations:

INTRODUCTION

BODY

CONCLUSION

- **Set up the quotation.** Provide a description or analysis before the quotation to tell readers what idea the quotation supports.
  *He sneezed so hard that he blew the house down by accident. "That's when my nose started to itch," he says. "I felt a sneeze coming on."*

- **Insert the quotation.** Integrate your own words with words from the story.
  *When we first meet him, the wolf is making a birthday cake for his "dear old granny."*

## Modeled Instruction

**Read the excerpt from "The Wolf's Side of the Story." Note the underlined details, and complete the activities to learn how the quotations support the writer's idea.**

### From MENTOR TEXT *page 93*

The wolf has the same explanation for what happened when he visited the house made of sticks. He describes the events of this encounter as an accident, which again shows that he didn't mean to hurt anybody. He probably would have said the same thing about the third house, but it was too strong to be taken down by a sneeze. The wolf explains that he only tried to break down the door because the pig inside had made a rude comment about his granny. "Now I'm usually a calm fellow," the wolf says. "But when somebody talks about my granny like that, I go a little crazy." From the wolf's point of view, he had every right to try to break down the door.

In his version of events, the wolf presents himself as completely innocent. He never changes his belief that the original story is "all wrong" and that his reputation is unfairly earned.

**1** Read the underlined quotation. In what way does the writer use this quotation in his paragraph?

_____

_____

_____

_____

**2** **Underline** another example of a quotation in the Mentor Text. Explain why you think the writer chose to use the quotation in this way.

_____

_____

_____

_____

## 👥 Guided Practice

Sweet T used his notes to write the draft below. Now he must find ways to further develop his ideas.

**Read Sweet T's notes and draft. Complete the activities, using the Hints for help.**

### Sweet T's Chart

| Encounter 1: Meeting in the Ocean | |
|---|---|
| Quotation | Analysis of Quotation |
| "How dare an Organic say that about me? She is the one with the dry, dull skin that does nothing but cover her body like an envelope." | The Teleote feels defensive. She insults the human's skin. This shows she thinks her skin is better than the human's. |
| "I feel an emotion I have never experienced before, one that makes me hot and tense inside." | The Teleote feels anger and discomfort. She does not like the humans. |

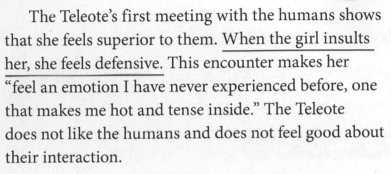

### Sweet T's Draft

   The Teleote's first meeting with the humans shows that she feels superior to them. <u>When the girl insults her, she feels defensive.</u> This encounter makes her "feel an emotion I have never experienced before, one that makes me hot and tense inside." The Teleote does not like the humans and does not feel good about their interaction.

**3** Read the underlined sentence in Sweet T's draft. How can Sweet T improve this sentence with a quotation from his notes? Explain your answer.

_____

_____

> **HINT** Use the Analysis of Quotation section of the chart to guide you.

**4** **Underline** the sentence in Sweet T's draft that includes a quotation. Do you think Sweet T uses this quotation successfully? Explain your answer.

_____

_____

> **HINT** Read the sentence aloud. Does it make sense?

💬 **Turn and Talk** Read aloud a paragraph from your essay, and have your partner listen for places where you can better support an idea with a quotation. Discuss the best way to add the quotation.

### Write Time ✏️

Finish drafting the body of your essay. Then draft a conclusion using the tips from the chart on page 110 for help.

# Step 6 Revise: First Read

**W.5.4:** Produce clear and coherent writing in which the development and organization are appropriate to task, purpose, and audience.

**W.5.5:** With guidance and support from peers and adults, develop and strengthen writing as needed by . . . revising. . . .

**FOCUS** Organization and Elaboration

As you revise, use your Literary Analysis Writing Checklist to check your writing. Work through the checklist, one line at a time. Reread the related parts of your essay to decide whether you did your best possible work for each trait described. In this step, you will practice checking your essay for three of the traits in the categories of Organization and Elaboration.

## Modeled Instruction

The Mentor Text writer, Philip Yee, used the same checklist to evaluate his draft.

**Read his Think Aloud to see how he checks his essay.**

### MENTOR TEXT Draft

The wolf's point of view also affects how he describes his three encounters with the pigs. According to the wolf, he just had a bad cold that day. When he came to the house made of straw to borrow sugar for granny's cake, he sneezed so hard that he blew the house down by accident. He has the same explanation for what happened when he visited the house made of sticks. He describes the events of this encounter as an accident, which again shows that he didn't mean to hurt anybody. He probably would have said the same thing about the third house, but it was too strong to be taken down by a sneeze.

In his version of events, the wolf presents himself as completely innocent. He never changes his belief that the original story is "all wrong" and that his reputation is unfairly earned.

It's hard not to like the wolf in the story when he tells it himself, but all you have to do is read the original to get a very different picture of what happened.

### Think Aloud

● **Organization** Are my details presented in a logical order? This part of my essay tells how the wolf's point of view affects the way he describes his encounters with the pigs. My details are in the same order as the events of the story. I think my readers will be able to follow the order of events the way I present them.

● **Elaboration** Do I include enough evidence to support each idea? Let's see. In a literary analysis essay, quotations are an important type of evidence, but I have only quoted a short phrase. I will add some quotations showing what happens when the wolf encounters the pigs and how the wolf thinks his reputation is unfairly earned. These quotations will make my analysis more convincing.

● **Organization** Does my conclusion sum up my analysis? Not really. Right now, I leave readers with a thoughtful idea. I'll add a sentence to the beginning of the paragraph that clearly sums up my analysis. It will say, "*The True Story of the Three Little Pigs!* shows that a narrator's point of view can greatly affect the way events and descriptions of other characters are presented."

Read the excerpt below from Sweet T's draft of the assignment. Then complete the activities. Use the Hints for help.

### Sweet T's Draft

The Teleote's point of view that she is better than humans influences how she describes her second and third encounters with humans. During the second encounter, she describes a party as an activity that doesn't make sense. The third encounter shows her belief that humans are physically weaker than Teleotes.

The Teleote's point of view toward humans does change. At the start, she believes she is better than humans in all ways. Toward the end, she thinks she has found new friends. She wants to get to know more about the humans.

The Teleote's experience with humans reminds us that we should never judge a book by its cover. If we get to know someone, we may change our minds.

**1 Organization** Does Sweet T present his ideas and details in a logical order? Explain your answer.

> **HINT** Look for words in his draft that show time order.

_____

_____

**2 Elaboration** Sweet T does not include enough evidence to support his ideas. Suggest ways that Sweet T can revise his draft to include more evidence.

> **HINT** What kind of evidence makes a literary analysis strong?

_____

_____

**3 Organization** How well does Sweet T's conclusion sum up his analysis? If needed, suggest a specific revision to help Sweet T improve his conclusion.

> **HINT** Does the conclusion tell you what the essay was all about?

_____

_____

**Turn and Talk** Take turns reading your body paragraphs aloud. Does each paragraph provide enough evidence to support the main idea?

### Write Time ✏

Use the Literary Analysis Writing Checklist passed out by your teacher to evaluate your draft for **Ideas**, **Organization**, and **Elaboration**.

# Step 7 Revise: Second Read

**W.5.2c:** Link ideas within and across categories of information using words, phrases, and clauses (e.g., *in contrast, especially*)

**W.5.5:** With guidance and support from peers and adults, develop and strengthen writing as needed by . . . revising. . . .

**FOCUS** Linking Words, Phrases, and Clauses

In this step, you'll look for ways to connect important ideas and make your essay flow smoothly. One way to do this is by using **linking words**, **phrases**, **and clauses**.

The chart below shows some examples you can use when writing a literary analysis essay.

| Linking Words, Phrases, and Clauses | | | |
|---|---|---|---|
| **Show Contrast** | **Show Elaboration** | **Show Emphasis** | **Show Cause and Effect** |
| • in contrast<br>• despite | • for instance<br>• in addition | • especially<br>• it is important to note | • as a result<br>• therefore |

As you revise your essay for language, ask yourself: *Can a reader follow each of my ideas from one to the next? Can I add a word, phrase, or clause to show the connection?*

## Modeled Instruction

**Read the following excerpt from "The Wolf's Side of the Story." Note how Philip Yee used linking words, phrases, and clauses to connect ideas. Then complete the activities.**

**From MENTOR TEXT** *page 92*

The original story of "The Three Little Pigs" is told by a narrator who describes the wolf as a "big, bad" animal. The pigs, on the other hand, are portrayed as innocent victims of a wolf who wants to blow their houses down and eat them for lunch. But in *The True Story of the Three Little Pigs!*, it's the wolf's turn to tell the story, and he clearly states his point of view. For instance, right at the beginning, he says, "I don't know how this whole Big Bad Wolf thing got started, but it's all wrong." This sentence sets up the rest of the story, in which we see all of the events from the wolf's point of view.

**1** Why does Philip use the underlined linking phrase?

_____

_____

**2** What linking word or phrase could Philip have used instead of the underlined word *But*? Suggest a replacement below.

_____

**3** **Draw a box** around the linking phrase that shows Philip is adding information about the wolf's point of view.

Read the following paragraph from an early draft of the Mentor Text. Then use the Hints to complete the activities that follow.

**MENTOR TEXT  Draft**

The wolf sees himself as kind. He shares information that readers didn't get in the original story. When we first meet him, the wolf is making a birthday cake for his "dear old granny." This makes the wolf seem thoughtful and caring, not big and bad.

**4** Philip wants to show a contrast between how the wolf sees himself and how he is portrayed in the original story of "The Three Little Pigs." Which of the following sentences expresses that idea most clearly? Circle the correct answer.

> **HINT** Use the chart on page 116 to guide you.

**A** Despite the way he has been portrayed, the wolf sees himself as kind.

**B** As a result of the way he has been portrayed, the wolf sees himself as kind.

**C** It is important to note how the wolf has been portrayed and how he sees himself as kind.

**D** In addition to the way he has been portrayed, the wolf sees himself as kind and caring.

**5** Philip wants to connect the underlined sentence to the sentence before it. Which phrase would best show the connection between these two sentences? Circle the correct answer.

> **HINT** How are the ideas in the two sentences related?

**A** In contrast

**B** In addition

**C** As a result

**D** For instance

💬 **Turn and Talk**  Take turns reading your essays aloud. Do the ideas flow smoothly? Discuss which linking words, phrases, or clauses could make your writing clearer.

**Write Time** 🖉

Use the Literary Analysis Writing Checklist passed out by your teacher to evaluate your draft for **Language**.

# Step 8 Edit for Conventions

**W.5.5:** With guidance and support from peers and adults, develop and strengthen writing as needed by . . . editing.

**L.5.1d:** Recognize and correct inappropriate shifts in verb tense.

**FOCUS** Shifts in Verb Tense

The last step is to make sure that your spelling, grammar, and punctuation are correct. In this step, you'll focus on correcting inappropriate shifts in verb tense.

**Verb tenses** show whether an event occurs in the past, the present, or the future. The following chart shows examples of verbs in each tense.

| Past Tense | Present Tense | Future Tense |
|---|---|---|
| I **saw** my friend. | I **see** my friend. | I **will see** my friend. |
| He **ate** a cookie. | He **eats** a cookie. | He **will eat** a cookie. |
| They **watched** a play. | They **watch** a play. | They **will watch** a play. |

In a literary analysis essay, story events are usually described in the present tense.

**Language Handbook** To learn more about shifts in verb tense, turn to page 194.

## Modeled Instruction

**Read the following excerpt from a draft of "The Wolf's Side of the Story."**
**Then complete the activities.**

**MENTOR TEXT** Draft

The original story of "The Three Little Pigs" is told by a narrator who described the wolf as a "big, bad" animal. The pigs were portrayed as innocent victims of a wolf who wants to blow their houses down. But in *The True Story of the Three Little Pigs!*, it will be the wolf's turn to talk. He started out showing his point of view by saying, "I don't know how this whole Big Bad Wolf thing got started, but it's all wrong." This sentence had set up the rest of the story, which shows the events from the wolf's point of view.

**1** In the first two sentences, the underlined verbs are in an incorrect tense. **Cross out** the verbs. Then **write** the correct form of the verb above each incorrect form.

**2** The rest of the paragraph has three incorrect shifts in verb tense. **Cross out** each verb with an incorrect form. Then **write** the correct form of the verb above the incorrect form.

## Guided Practice

**Read the following excerpt from an early draft of "The Wolf's Side of the Story."**
**Then complete the activities. Use the Hints for help.**

**MENTOR TEXT** Draft

The wolf will be explaining that he only tried to break down the door because the pig inside had made a rude comment about his granny. "Now I'm usually a calm fellow," the wolf had said, "but when somebody talks about my granny like that I go a little crazy."

**3** Read this sentence from the draft:

The wolf <u>will be explaining</u> that he only tried to break down the door because the pig inside had made a rude comment about his granny.

Which word or words should replace the underlined verb to make the sentence correct? Circle the correct answer.

**A** will explain

**B** explained

**C** explains

**D** had explained

> **HINT** In what tense are events described in a literary analysis essay?

**4** Read this sentence from the draft:

"Now I'm usually a calm fellow," the wolf <u>had said</u>, "but when somebody talks about my granny like that I go a little crazy."

On the lines below, rewrite the sentence, replacing the underlined words with the correct verb tense.

> **HINT** What are the different forms of the verb *to say*?

_____

_____

**Turn and Talk** Take turns reading aloud paragraphs from your essays. Are there any confusing shifts in verb tense? If so, discuss which verbs should be changed to the present tense.

**Write Time** 🖉

Use the Literary Analysis Writing Checklist passed out by your teacher to evaluate your draft for **Conventions**.

# Writing to Inform: Book Chapter

**W.5.2:** Write informative/explanatory texts to examine a topic and convey ideas and information clearly.

**W.5.7:** Conduct short research projects that use several sources to build knowledge through investigation of different aspects of a topic.

## Sharing Information

Robbie's class is writing a book about mammals—animals that have backbones and nurse their young. Each student will write a chapter, but Robbie can't decide which mammal to write about.

During a trip to the zoo, Robbie becomes fascinated by a family of hamadryas baboons, a type of monkey from the northeastern part of Africa. The baboons act in some very humanlike ways: a mother makes lip-smacking sounds to her baby, and a male seems to call, "Wahoo!" Robbie decides to write his chapter on the baboons so he can show others just how interesting these creatures are.

By writing an informational chapter, Robbie aims to teach readers something new about the world around them. Read the excerpt from Robbie's chapter below. What have you learned about hamadryas baboons?

4:15 PM                                                          90%

Hamadryas baboons travel together in a pack called a *harem*. Each harem has several females and one or two males. Sometimes harems will join together into *clans*. This can make the tough job of finding food a little easier.

Hamadryas baboons also make some curious sounds. The male gives a bark that sounds like "Wahoo!" It signals danger or warns other males to . . .

**The male hamadryas baboon has lighter fur than the female.**

# What Is Informational Writing?

Informational writing teaches or explains a topic to readers. The writer uses facts, definitions, quotations, and examples—often from research—to develop the topic.

## KEY FEATURES · Informational Writing

- an introduction that states the topic clearly and prepares readers to learn about the topic
- facts and details that are logically organized in paragraphs
- precise language and domain-specific vocabulary that express ideas concisely and accurately
- linking words, phrases, and clauses that connect one idea to the next
- a conclusion that restates the topic, sums up the important points, and leaves readers with something to think about

## Steps for Writing

On the following pages, you'll learn the steps for writing your own book chapter.

The Research Path

| Step 1 | Study a Mentor Text | Step 5 | Draft Your Book Chapter |
| Step 2 | Unpack Your Assignment | Step 6 | Revise: First Read |
| Step 3 | Find Text Evidence | Step 7 | Revise: Second Read |
| Step 4 | Organize Your Evidence | Step 8 | Edit for Conventions |

# Step 1  Study a Mentor Text

Before you write your book chapter, you'll study a model. First, read to understand what it's about. Then reread to understand how it was written.

**As you reread the Mentor Text, do the numbered activities. They'll help you understand the key features of a book chapter.**

> **MENTOR TEXT: Book Chapter**
>
> # Hiding in Plain Sight
>
> *by Caleb Lawrence*
>
> 1    For an animal in the wild, threats to survival are everywhere. All habitats have risks. For example, water sources can dry up. Food can grow scarce. The weather can turn dangerous without warning. But perhaps most worrisome to animals is the constant danger of becoming another animal's lunch. To avoid being eaten by hungry predators (or better yet, to stalk their own prey!), many animals use **camouflage**—the natural coloring or shape of their bodies which allows them to disappear into their surroundings. There are three main types of animal camouflage.
>
> ## True Colors
>
> 2    The first type of camouflage is coloration. According to *Encyclopedia Britannica*, **concealing coloration** lets an animal hide against a background of the same color. For example, Arctic hares live in the North American tundra. During winter, their coats turn white so they can blend in with the snowy environment, making them less visible to predators. In the spring, their coats return to a blue-gray color that matches the rocks and plant life around them. Owls also rely on concealing coloration. During the day, when predators are lurking, owls sleep snugly in tree burrows. Their brown feathers blend seamlessly into the tree trunk.
>
> 3    Animals with **disruptive coloration**, such as zebras, are colored in a way that makes the outline of their bodies hard to see. Because zebras tend to travel in groups, predators struggle to identify a single zebra to attack amongst the sea of black and white stripes. Animals that rely on disruptive coloration for hunting include Sumatran tigers and jaguars.

**1** **Introduction**  In paragraph 1, **draw a dashed line** under the sentences that tell what topic the book chapter will inform readers about.

**2** **Headings**  Explain why the writer organizes his chapter with headings.

_____

_____

_____

_____

**3** **Develop the Topic**  The writer introduces four kinds of camouflage in paragraphs 2–5. **Underline** the sentence in each paragraph that defines the type of camouflage.

A tiger's stripes make it hard for prey to recognize its shape when moving through tall grasses. Jaguars hunt during the day in the low-lying leaves of tree branches. Their splotchy markings keep them from standing out amid the shifting patterns of light and shade.

## The Art of Disguise

4    The second type of camouflage is **disguise**. This is similar to concealing coloration because it helps animals blend in with their surroundings. But when an animal is disguised, it relies on its shape or texture to keep it safe, not just its color. For example, certain tree frogs look like lumps of velvety, green moss. Additionally, the walking leaf insect perfectly matches the shape, texture, and color of the plant leaves in its habitat. And the lantern fly, which lives on tree trunks, is rough, scaly, and brown like tree bark.

## Magnificent Mimicry

5    The third type of camouflage is **mimicry**. In this case, the animal that wants to avoid being eaten copies certain characteristics of an animal that the predator does not want to eat. For example, a hawk will not eat monarch butterflies because they are toxic to birds. As a result, the viceroy butterfly has grown to look a lot like a monarch butterfly, which is a useful characteristic to have when facing a bird of prey. Owl butterflies also rely on mimicry to stay safe. These unusual butterflies have enormous spots on their wings that look like the eyes of an owl. When threatened, the owl butterfly spreads its wings and takes flight. Consequently, its stalker is frightened, giving the butterfly time to escape.

6    Not all animals are able to use camouflage to keep themselves safe. But those that can take advantage of coloration, disguise, and mimicry are likely to live longer in the wild than those that can't. The next time you walk past a fallen tree branch or a leafy green plant, take a close look. You never know what might be hiding there!

7    **Sources**

"Camouflage." National Geographic Education. www.nationalgeographic.com

"Concealing coloration." *Encyclopedia Britannica Online*

"Critter Camouflage." Sacramento Zoo. www.saczoo.org

**4 Linking Words, Phrases & Clauses** In paragraphs 4 and 5, the writer uses several linking words, phrases, and clauses to connect ideas. **Draw a box** around the words and phrases that show examples of a concept. Then **circle** the words and phrases that show cause and effect.

**5 Conclusion** In paragraph 6, the writer connects his conclusion to an important idea in his introduction. **Draw a dashed line** beneath the sentence that makes this connection.

**6 Sources** Why do you think the writer provides a list of sources at the end of his chapter?

_____

_____

_____

**W.5.4:** Produce clear and coherent writing in which the development and organization are appropriate to task, purpose, and audience.

# Step 2 Unpack Your Assignment

**FOCUS** Identify Task, Purpose, and Audience

Before you begin writing, read your assignment carefully to identify your task, purpose, and audience. Remember that in informational writing, your **purpose** is to examine a topic and convey ideas and information clearly.

To do this well, you must consider how much your **audience** might, or might not, know about the topic. Understanding your audience will help you decide whether to define particular words or provide important background information for concepts that are likely to be unfamiliar to your readers.

## Modeled Instruction

Caleb Lawrence, who wrote "Hiding in Plain Sight" on pages 122–123, was given the assignment below. He read it carefully and marked up some important details.

**Read Caleb's assignment. Then read the points in his Think Aloud, which tell how he identified his audience, task, and purpose.**

### CALEB'S Assignment

Your local zoo has invited students to write and submit short informational texts about various animal traits. The best texts will be published as chapters in a book that will be handed out to zoo visitors of all ages. You will write your chapter about camouflage and tell why it is important to animal survival.

In your book chapter:

- Describe three types of camouflage that animals have or use.
- Provide examples of animals that have or use each type of camouflage.
- Explain why camouflage is important to animal survival.

Use headings to organize your information, and provide a list of sources.

### Think Aloud

- **Purpose** The word *informational* tells my purpose for writing: to *inform*, or provide facts and details about a topic. I want my audience to learn from what I write.

- **Audience** The phrase *zoo visitors* tells me that my audience wants to learn about animals. The phrase *of all ages* means that both kids and adults might read this book. I'll be sure to define words that might be hard for kids and use good examples to make my ideas very clear to everyone.

- **Task** These bullets show what information I need to include in my chapter. I wonder how I might organize all of this information. The word *three* gives me an idea: maybe I'll start by describing one type of camouflage, and tell more about it by giving examples and then explaining why it's important to animal survival. This way I can create one heading for each type of camouflage. The list of sources at the end will tell my readers that my information is reliable.

## 👥 Guided Practice

**Now it's your turn to write a book chapter. Read Your Assignment carefully. Then complete the activities, using the Hints for help.**

### Your Assignment ✏️

Your science class is writing an informational book about animals that will be displayed in your school library. Each student must write one short chapter for the book. Your chapter will describe some purposes for animal communication and explain how that communication helps the animals survive.

**To prepare to write your chapter, you will read the following sources:**

- Incredible Animal Ears  *page 130*
- Dances with Animals  *pages 131–137*

**In your book chapter:**

- Identify three purposes for animal communication.
- Provide one or more examples of ways that animals commuunciate for each purpose.
- Explain why communication is important to animal survival.

Use headings to organize your information, and provide a list of sources.

> *Hi, I'm Bella, and I'm also going to be doing this assignment.*

**1** **Audience** **Draw a box** around the phrase that tells about your audience. Then explain who your readers will most likely be.

> **HINT** Who visits the place where the book will be displayed?

**2** **Purpose** **Draw a dashed line** beneath the detail that tells your purpose for writing.

> **HINT** What type of book is your science class writing?

**3** **Task** **Underline** the information you need to include in your book chapter. Then explain how you might organize this information.

> **HINT** How did Caleb Lawrence organize "Hiding in Plain Sight"?

💬 **Turn and Talk** Why is it important to provide a list of your sources?

# The Research Path
## Writing from Sources

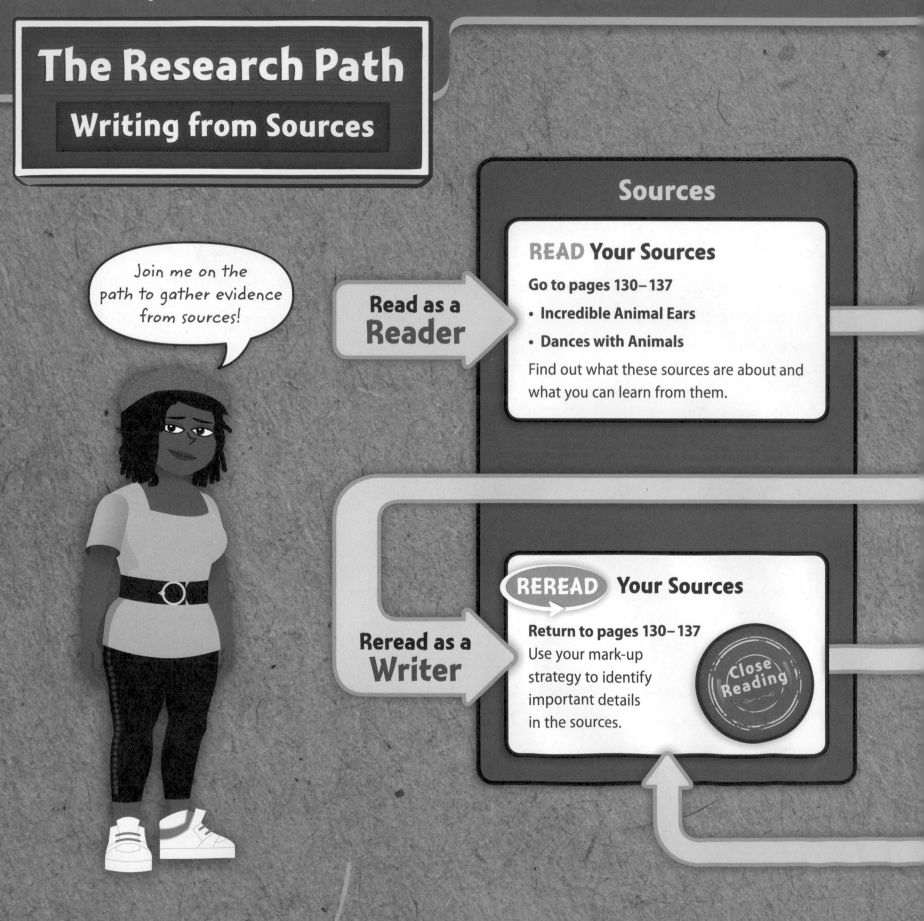

Join me on the path to gather evidence from sources!

**Read as a Reader**

**Sources**

### READ Your Sources

Go to pages 130–137

- **Incredible Animal Ears**
- **Dances with Animals**

Find out what these sources are about and what you can learn from them.

**Reread as a Writer**

### REREAD Your Sources

**Return to pages 130–137**
Use your mark-up strategy to identify important details in the sources.

Close Reading

## REVIEW Your Assignment

**Return to page 125**
Reread your task to
identify the types
of information you
will need to include
in your book chapter.

# Text Evidence

## FIND Text Evidence

**Go to pages 128–129**
Learn how to mark
important details
so you can find
them quickly later on.

## THINK It Through

**Go to pages 138–139**
Complete the activities
to help you connect
the ideas in the sources
to your assignment.

## ORGANIZE Your Evidence

**Go to pages 140–141**
Use a chart to
group your ideas
and evidence so
that you're ready
to write.

**Need More
Information?**

**Begin Writing!**
**Go to pages 142–143**

W.5.8: . . . gather relevant information from print . . . sources. . . .

# Step 3 Find Text Evidence

FOCUS Gather information

You've unpacked your assignment and identified the information you need to include in your chapter. As you reread your sources, look for details that will help you explain animal communication. Begin by looking for the first two ideas from your assignment:

- **The purpose for communication.** Why do animals interact within and between groups? What message do they want to send, and why? Mark these details with a **P**, for *purpose*. Then briefly label the purpose (for example, *P-territory*).

- **Examples of animals communicating.** How do the animals behave? Why do they communicate this way? Mark these details with an **E**, for *example*. Then label which purpose the example describes (for example, *E-territory*).

As you identify each purpose for communication, think about the third idea in your assignment—why that form of communication is important to animal survival. If the source texts don't state the reason why, then you will need to make an inference.

## Modeled Instruction

To gather information for her book chapter, Bella marked up the text as she read the source, "Dances with Animals."

**Read the text and Bella's Think Aloud to learn more about the reading and mark-up strategies she used.**

From **"Dances with Animals"** *page 132*
*P-share information*

    As she traces a figure 8 on the dance floor, the follower bees touch her with their antennae. They sense the odors of apple blossom nectar and pollen clinging to her body. These workers also detect the scent she used to mark the distant flowers. <u>A flight plan is coded in her movements.</u> The length of the waggle run tells workers how far the flowers are from the hive. Its angle tells them how to get there. Because bees steer by the sun, the dancer links her directions to its position in the sky.
*E-share information*

### Think Aloud

● In this paragraph, a bee is doing a dance of some sort. The text says "A flight plan is coded in her movements." Other bees are using her movements and her scent to get information about where she has found some flowers. So this paragraph is definitely about animals communicating for a purpose: to share information. I'll mark it with a P and label it *share information*.

● The bees are an example of animals that communicate to share information, so I'll also mark and label this paragraph with *E-share information*.

● This paragraph doesn't explain why sharing information is important to survival, but in this case they're sharing information about food. Every animal needs food to survive!

**Read the following excerpt from "Dances with Animals." Then complete the activities, using the Hints for help.**

From **"Dances with Animals"** *page 133*

Most fish settle conflicts over territory without fighting. But Siamese fighting fish, also know as bettas, are little fish with a big mean streak. Brightly colored bettas in pet stores have been specially bred for their beautiful veil-like fins. In the wild, they live in rice paddies in southeast Asia.

If threatened, male Siamese fighting fish switch back and forth between face-to-face and side-to-side positions. Facing each other, they flare out flaps of skin on their necks and extend their fins. This makes them seem twice their size. Side-to-side, they flicker their fins and beat the water with their tails. Tail beating gets faster and faster until one male backs down. The loser lowers his fins and puts his tail down. His bright red, blue, or purple body color fades to a dull hue. Defeated, he swims away.

**1** The first paragraph of the excerpt states one purpose for animal communication. **Underline** the purpose. Then **mark** it with a P and briefly **label** it.

> **HINT** How does the paragraph contrast bettas with "most fish"?

**2** **Underline** details that show an example of animals communicating. **Mark** and **label** the purpose it describes. Then summarize the details below.

> **HINT** How does one fish become a winner and the other a loser?

_____

_____

**3** Does the excerpt tell how this kind of animal communication helps the bettas survive? If so, record the evidence below. If not, make an inference.

> **HINT** Why might a fish want to avoid getting into an actual fight?

_____

_____

💬 **Turn and Talk** How will using markups to distinguish between different types of information be helpful when you're doing research for informational writing?

# INCREDIBLE ANIMAL EARS

**by Charles Rollins**

1   Elephants storm across a hot, African desert toward a source of water. Suddenly, they stop. Their ears open up wide and appear to hear distinct sounds, and yet humans observing the scene nearby hear nothing. What is happening? Actually, the elephants are hearing a sound, but it has a pitch so low that humans can't detect it. We call this low pitch infrasound.

2   Scientists finally discovered this sound by using a machine called a spectrograph. This machine charted the sounds so scientists could study them along with the elephants' behaviors. These scientists concluded that the low sounds were actually warning sounds from another herd.

3   The deepest rumbling sounds measure between 1 and 20 hertz, way below the sounds that human ears can detect. These infrasonic calls can mean different things, such as "Hello, I'm here," "Help, I'm lost," "Keep away," or "Danger ahead."

4   Scientists continue to study the sounds that elephants make, and it's no easy task. So far, they have discovered about 70 different sounds that they use for different situations.

# Dances with Animals

by Ellen R. Braaf, Ask

1   A honey bee returns to the hive. Sticky pollen clings to her body. Nectar fills her honey sac. She's found apple blossoms in a distant orchard. How does she tell other worker bees about this new food source? She dances!

2   Unlike humans, animals don't have words to help them communicate. They can't say "Hey! Look what I found," or "Keep away! This is my spot," or "Want to go steady?" Yet, animals communicate all the time. They send out signals—messages others receive and understand using their senses of smell, taste, touch, hearing, and sight.

3   Animals with good vision "talk" to each other with their bodies. They use patterns of movements to share information, to defend themselves or their territories, and to attract mates. Nature designs their steps, and they dance as if their lives depended on it. Often, they do.

## Language of Bees

4 Most communication takes place among members of the same species. In dark beehives, honeycombed walls become waxy dance floors. Like a rock star swarmed by adoring fans, a bee returning from the apple orchard begins her dance. Other workers follow her as she moves forward in a straight line. She vibrates her wings and wags her body side to side very quickly—13 to 15 times a second. Then she turns to one side, circles back, and begins the waggle run again. When she finishes, she circles around—this time in the opposite direction—and repeats her steps. The dance may go on for hours.

5 As she traces a figure 8 on the dance floor, the follower bees touch her with their antennae. They sense the odors of apple blossom nectar and pollen clinging to her body. These workers also detect the scent she used to mark the distant flowers. A flight plan is coded in her movements. The length of the waggle run tells workers how far the flowers are from the hive. Its angle tells them how to get there. Because bees steer by the sun, the dancer links her directions to its position in the sky.

6 However, the position of the sun in the sky keeps changing. If the waggle dance lasts for hours, how do bees leaving the hive long after the dance has begun find their targets? Amazingly, they do. The waggling bee adjusts her dance to account for the sun's movement.

**Honey bees**

# KEEP AWAY! "This is my spot!"

7    Not all animals cooperate the way honey bees do. Most compete for food, territory and mates. Fights take time and energy. Rivals risk injury and death, weakening the group as a whole. So some animals dance instead, using movements to make themselves look larger, stronger, and quicker than their competition. "Don't mess with me," they say.

## Red Fish, Blue Fish

8    Most fish settle conflicts over territory without fighting. But Siamese fighting fish, also know as bettas, are little fish with a big mean streak. Brightly colored bettas in pet stores have been specially bred for their beautiful veil-like fins. In the wild, they live in rice paddies in southeast Asia.

9    If threatened, male Siamese fighting fish switch back and forth between face-to-face and side-to-side positions. Facing each other, they flare out flaps of skin on their necks and extend their fins. This makes them seem twice their size. Side-to-side, they flicker their fins and beat the water with their tails. Tail beating gets faster and faster until one male backs down. The loser lowers his fins and puts his tail down. His bright red, blue, or purple body color fades to a dull hue. Defeated, he swims away.

**Siamese fighting fish**

## Lizard Lingo

10    Lizards sport a wide variety of odd body parts: scaly crests on their tails, necks, and backs; spines, knobs, and horns on their heads; and fleshy dewlaps—flaps of skin under their necks that flare out like fans, then disappear. When males compete for territory or challenge each other to see who is "the best," these weird ornaments come in handy.

11    Green anoles are small lizards found in the southeastern United States. They cling to rocks, trees, walls, and screens. At times, it looks as if they're listening to hip-hop music on invisible headsets. Their bodies groove to the beat. Their heads bob as their legs push up and down.

12    When two male anoles meet, they really get going. To appear bigger and scarier, they raise a scaly ridge or crest along their backs and develop dark spots behind their eye sockets. They turn to the side to present the broadest part of their bodies to each other. The dance ends when one backs down.

13    The loser bobs his head slowly as if to say "you the man," then moves away.

Green anole in the Florida Keys

## Spectacular Spiders

14    With their eight legs, wolf spiders have a hairy "chorus line" attached to their bodies. When males meet, they challenge each other. They move back and forth, raising their brush-covered forelegs, and waving their palps, jawlike feelers. One spider lunges; the other backs away. If they're evenly matched, they may switch roles and the fleeing male becomes the chaser. As they run, retreat, approach, wave their abdomens, make contact, and tap each other, their dance looks like a cross between a cha-cha and a boxing match.

Wolf spider

# High Jumpers

15    On the plains of Africa, deerlike antelopes such as gazelles and impalas perform a remarkable dance step to discourage predators. Sometimes, when a cheetah is about to attack, one gazelle bounds up and down, jumping into the air with back arched and legs stiff. This behavior, called stotting or pronking, puzzles scientists. Why would a gazelle, about to become dinner, waste time jumping around instead of high-tailing it out of there?

16    Some scientists think these gazelles are warning the rest of the herd. Others believe that by leaping into the air in the face of danger, stotting gazelles are sending attackers a signal. It says, "Nanny nanny, boo boo. I'm not scared of you. I'm fit and fast. You'll never catch me." As cheetahs usually attack the weakest animals in the herd, catching a gazelle with enough energy to jump so high might be too much work.

17    Meerkats use pronking to defend their territory. These desert-dwelling cousins of the mongoose are well known for their ability to stand up straight on their hind legs to keep watch for predators. When rival bands threaten, however, they perform a "war dance," jumping up and down and jeering loudly. The group moves forward and then stops, each animal pawing the ground like crazy. They hope that the rising dust and confusion are enough to drive the invaders away.

**Alert meerkats keeping watch**

**Herd of South African impala jumping and pronking**

# CHANCE FOR ROMANCE:
# "Do you want to go steady?"

18    The displays males use when threatened can be a lot like the moves they use when trying to get a mate. That's probably because they're signaling similar things, such as strength and power. When courting females, their signals might say, "Hey! You over there. Look at me. I'm big and strong. I'll be a great mate. I'll protect you and our offspring. I'll provide food and shelter. Pick me."

19    Choosing a healthy, strong, clever partner is important. It means that animals have a better chance to pass their genes on to the next generation. Some animals meet only to mate. Some raise their young together. Others bond for life. Of the many courtship dances among animals, birds do some of the most interesting.

**Great crested grebes in mating season**

## Water Ballet

20    Great crested grebes do a complicated water ballet. Facing each other, they shake their heads and bend their long slender necks. They skim across the surface of a lake together, dive into the water, then rise at the same time with weeds in their beaks. Then they shake their heads, showing off the ruffs and tufts of feathers that adorn them. They tread water and dance with weeds dangling from their beaks. Sometimes, they'll fling aside their grassy gifts and start again. This togetherness dance helps them be better mates and parents.

## Strutting Their Stuff

21    Some kinds of birds perform their courtship dances all together at gatherings called leks. The males put up with the competition because leks attract lots of females—far more than a single male could. Females flock to leks to see potential mates strut their stuff. Some take their time choosing and come back several days in a row.

22    Sage grouse are large, chicken-like birds of the American plains. In spring, they gather in openings in the sagebrush about the size of football fields. To attract females, males flair out their long, pointy tail feathers to form a speckled fan. With chests puffed up and air sacs inflated, they parade around making soft drumming and popping noises. These dances may go on long into the night if there's enough moonlight.

**Male greater sage grouse struts and dances**

## The Show-Off

23    Some birds dance alone on smaller stages. More than 40 different kinds of birds of paradise live on the island of New Guinea. The male six-plumed bird of paradise does an energetic dance to impress any watching females. First he cleans leaves off his stage, the dimly lit forest floor. Then he fluffs out a fancy ruff of special neck feathers and hops sideways, bobbing his head. In a final showy move, he wiggles his six plumes. If his dance has impressed one of the watching females, it may mean the beginning of a new romance.

**Bird of paradise**

## Think It Through

**Use details from your sources to complete the following activities. Your responses will help you write your book chapter.**

**1** On page 131 of "Dances with Animals," the text states that animals "dance as if their lives depended on it. Often, they do." Explain what this statement means, using at least three examples from this article.

> **HINT** What do your sources tell you about the different kinds of threats animals face in the wild?

_____

_____

_____

_____

_____

_____

_____

_____

_____

_____

_____

**2** Describe two examples of the way that animals use sound to communicate. Then describe two examples of the way that animals use movement to communicate.

HINT Remember that animals can communicate through both sound and movement.

_____

_____

_____

_____

_____

_____

**3** Review the details you marked with a P in your sources. On the lines below, list every purpose for animal communication that you identified.

_____

_____

_____

_____

_____

How many examples did you label for each purpose? Choose the three purposes with the most examples. Then on the lines above, draw a star beside the three purposes you will discuss in your book chapter.

HINT Look at each example. Do you have enough information about how and why the animal communicates?

# Step 4 Organize Your Evidence

**W.5.5:** With guidance and support from peers and adults, develop and strengthen writing as needed by planning....

**W.5.8:** ...summarize or paraphrase information in notes....

**FOCUS** Plan Your Book Chapter

Now that you've gathered information from your sources, it's time to organize it. Group each purpose for animal communication with examples that illustrate or explain the purpose more completely. Then provide a brief explanation for how each type of communication helps the animals survive. Each purpose and its supporting information will be a section in your book chapter.

## Modeled Instruction

To organize her ideas and examples, Bella created the chart below. She added a detail from her first source "Incredible Animal Ears." Now she needs to add details from her second source, "Dances with Animals."

**Notice the organization of Bella's chart. Read the excerpt, and choose another example to support her purpose. Then make an inference to complete the last row.**

From **"Dances with Animals"** *page 132*
P-share information

    As she traces a figure 8 on the dance floor, the follower bees touch her with their antennae. They sense the odors of apple blossom nectar and pollen clinging to her body. These workers also detect the scent she used to mark the distant flowers. A flight plan is coded in her movements. The length of the waggle run tells workers how far the flowers are from the hive. Its angle tells them how to get there. Because bees steer by the sun, the dancer links her directions to its position in the sky.

E-share information

### Bella's Chart

| **Purpose:** Animals communicate to share information. | |
|---|---|
| Examples | • Elephants use low rumbling sounds to send messages to one another, including warnings. <br><br> • Honey bees _____ _____ _____ _____ |
| How This Helps Animal Survival | _____ _____ _____ _____ |

## Guided Practice

**Read the following excerpt from "Dances with Animals" and continue helping Bella to fill in her chart by completing the activities. Use the Hints for help.**

From **"Dances with Animals"** *page 134*

When two male anoles meet, they really get going To appear bigger and scarier, they raise a scaly ridge or crest along their backs and develop dark spots behind their eye sockets. They turn to the side to present the broadest part of their bodies to each other. The dance ends when one backs down. . . .

### Spectacular Spiders

With their eight legs, wolf spiders have a hairy "chorus line" attached to their bodies. When males meet, they challenge each other. They move back and forth, raising their brush-covered forelegs, and waving their palps, jawlike feelers. One spider lunges; the other backs away. If they're evenly matched, they may switch roles and the fleeing male becomes the chaser.

**Bella's Chart**

| **Purpose:** Animals communicate to defend themselves or their territory. | |
|---|---|
| Examples | • The anole morphs its body and turns itself in order to appear bigger. <br><br> • _____ <br><br> _____ <br><br> _____ |
| How This Helps Animal Survival | _____ <br><br> _____ <br><br> _____ |

1 Read the example in Bella's chart. **Underline** the details in the excerpt that Bella used to write this note in her chart.

2 Read the excerpt, and choose a second example of an animal communicating to defend itself or its territory. Write the example in the chart in your own words.

3 Explain how "dancing" instead of fighting helps animals survive. Write your explanation in the last row of the chart.

**Turn and Talk** Share any additional examples that you could use to support the purpose Bella wrote in this chart or in the chart on the previous page.

> **HINT** *Morphs* means "changes."

> **HINT** The heading signals that a new subject is beginning.

> **HINT** What would happen if animals always fought?

### Write Time

In your chart, record your purposes and the examples that support them. Then tell how each type of communication helps animal survival.

# Step 5 Draft Your Book Chapter

W.5.2: Write informative/explanatory texts to examine a topic and convey ideas and information clearly....

W.5.2a: Introduce a topic clearly and group related information logically; include formatting (e.g., headings)... when useful to aiding comprehension.

**FOCUS**  Write an Introduction

Read this chart to learn more about the parts of a book chapter. You can refer back to this information as you write your draft.

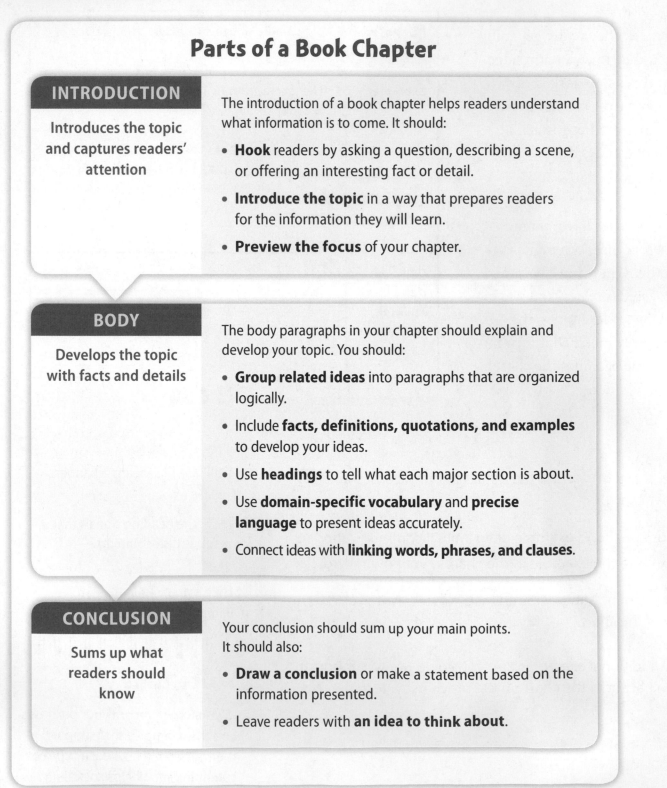

## Parts of a Book Chapter

**INTRODUCTION**

Introduces the topic and captures readers' attention

The introduction of a book chapter helps readers understand what information is to come. It should:

- **Hook** readers by asking a question, describing a scene, or offering an interesting fact or detail.
- **Introduce the topic** in a way that prepares readers for the information they will learn.
- **Preview the focus** of your chapter.

**BODY**

Develops the topic with facts and details

The body paragraphs in your chapter should explain and develop your topic. You should:

- **Group related ideas** into paragraphs that are organized logically.
- Include **facts, definitions, quotations, and examples** to develop your ideas.
- Use **headings** to tell what each major section is about.
- Use **domain-specific vocabulary** and **precise language** to present ideas accurately.
- Connect ideas with **linking words, phrases, and clauses**.

**CONCLUSION**

Sums up what readers should know

Your conclusion should sum up your main points. It should also:

- **Draw a conclusion** or make a statement based on the information presented.
- Leave readers with **an idea to think about**.

## Draft Your INTRODUCTION

Practice writing the different parts of your introduction. Study each example from the Mentor Text. Then try writing a similar part for your chapter.

INTRODUCTION

BODY

CONCLUSION

### Hook Your Readers

| Mentor Text | For an animal in the wild, threats to survival are everywhere. All habitats have risks. For example, water sources can dry up. Food can grow scarce. The weather can turn dangerous without warning. But perhaps most worrisome to animals is the constant danger of becoming another animal's lunch. |
|---|---|
| Your Chapter | |

**HINT** This hook ties into animal survival. What are some of your ideas about animal communication and survival?

### Introduce the Topic

| Mentor Text | To avoid being eaten by hungry predators (or better yet, to stalk their own prey!), many animals use camouflage—the natural coloring or shape of their bodies which allows them to disappear into their surroundings. |
|---|---|
| Your Chapter | |

**HINT** Notice how the Mentor Text provides a bridge between the hook and the main idea of the chapter.

### Preview the Main Ideas

| Mentor Text | There are three main types of animal camouflage. |
|---|---|
| Your Chapter | |

**HINT** What three purposes for communication will you focus on?

**Write Time** 🖉

Use your ideas from this page to draft your introduction. Then begin drafting your body paragraphs.

**Turn and Talk** Discuss other hooks you could use to get your readers interested in the topic of animal communication.

**W.5.2b:** Develop the topic with facts, definitions, concrete details, quotations, or other information and examples related to the topic.

**FOCUS** Use Concrete Details

## Draft Your BODY

As you draft your book chapter, you will develop your topic with facts, definitions, and concrete details from your sources. A **concrete detail** is specific, factual information that can be proved. Writers use concrete details such as specific descriptions, examples, or direct quotations, to help readers visualize what is being explained.

The following chart shows examples of nonspecfic details versus concrete details.

| Nonspecific Detail | Concrete Detail |
|---|---|
| Arctic hares change color. | During winter, the coat of an Arctic hare turns white to match the snow. |
| Owl butterflies have spots on their wings. | These unusual butterflies have enormous spots on their wings that look like the eyes of an owl. |

## 👥 Modeled Instruction

**Read the excerpt from "Hiding in Plain Sight." Then complete the activities to learn how the writer used concrete details to develop his ideas.**

**From MENTOR TEXT** *page 122*

Animals with **disruptive coloration**, such as zebras, are colored in a way that makes the outline of their bodies hard to see. Because zebras tend to travel in groups, <u>predators struggle to identify a single zebra to attack amongst the sea of black and white stripes.</u> Animals that rely on disruptive coloration for hunting include Sumatran tigers and jaguars. A tiger's stripes make it hard for prey to recognize its shape when moving through tall grasses. Jaguars hunt during the day in the low-lying leaves of tree branches. Their splotchy markings keep them from standing out amid the shifting patterns of light and shade.

**1** Why is the first underlined sentence a good example of a concrete detail?

_____

_____

**2** Underline an additional example of a concrete detail. Explain why you underlined this detail.

_____

_____

_____

Bella used her notes to write the draft below. Now she wants to find ways to develop her book chapter with concrete details.

**Read Bella's notes and draft. Complete the activities, using the Hints for help.**

**Bella's Chart**

| Purpose: Animals communicate to share information. | |
|---|---|
| Examples | • Elephants use low rumbling sounds to send messages to one another, including warnings. The sound is inaudible to humans.<br>• Honey bees do a careful dance to show the others where to find nearby flowers. The flight plan is coded in the bee's movements.<br>• Gazelles jump up and down with stiff legs (called "pronking") to warn of danger. |

**Bella's Draft**

One purpose for animal communication is sharing information. For example, elephants make sounds that can serve as warnings. Bees dance to share where to find food. Gazelles pronk to warn the herd when cheetahs are near.

**3** Bella mentions the sounds that elephants make. Rewrite her sentence on the lines below to show how she can improve this sentence with a concrete detail.

_____

_____

> **HINT** What else should readers know about the elephants' sounds?

**4** Bella's draft explains that "bees dance to share where to find food." Offer Bella a suggestion for how she can be more specific.

_____

_____

> **HINT** Sometimes you may also need to reread specific details in the source.

**5** Bella uses the word "pronk" in her third example. Explain how she can provide more concrete information for her readers.

_____

_____

> **HINT** Will this term be familiar to her readers?

**Turn and Talk** Why is it important to use concrete details when writing informational text?

**Write Time** ✏

Finish drafting the body of your book chapter. Then draft a conclusion using the tips from the chart on page 142 for help.

# Step 6 Revise: First Read

**W.5.4:** Produce clear and coherent writing in which the development and organization are appropriate to task, purpose, and audience.

**W.5.5:** With guidance and support from peers and adults, develop and strengthen writing as needed by . . . revising. . . .

**FOCUS** Organization and Elaboration

As you revise, use your Informational Writing Checklist to check your writing. Work through the checklist, one line at a time. Reread the related parts of your book chapter to decide whether you did your best possible work for each trait described. In this step, you will check your book chapter for three of the traits in the categories of Organization and Elaboration.

## Modeled Instruction

The Mentor Text writer, Caleb Lawrence, used the same checklist to evaluate his draft.

**Read his Think Aloud to see how he checks his book chapter.**

### MENTOR TEXT Draft

The first type of camouflage is coloration. **Concealing coloration** lets an animal hide against a background of the same color. For example, Arctic hares turn white in the winter so they can blend in with the snow. In the spring, they return to gray, which matches the rocks around them. A Sumatran tiger's stripes make it hard to see its shape when moving through tall grass. Owls sleep in tree burrows during the day, when predators are lurking. Their brown feathers blend into the tree trunk.

**Disruptive coloration** makes it difficult for other animals to see the outline of their bodies. The most famous example is probably zebra stripes, a popular pattern often used on furniture and decorations. Because zebras tend to travel in groups, it's not easy for a predator to identify a single zebra to attack. Jaguars hunt during the day in the low-lying leaves of tree branches. Their spots keep them from standing out amid the patterns of light and shade.

### Think Aloud

● **Organization** Did I group my main ideas with related facts, details, and examples? Let's see. My first paragraph is about concealing coloration. My examples are animals that have the same color as their background, except for the Sumatran tiger, which has stripes. Stripes are an example of disruptive coloration. I'll move this fact to the next paragraph, which deals with that type of camouflage.

● **Elaboration** Do all my details clearly relate to the topic? They should all tell about animal camouflage. The details in my first paragraph are all about camouflage. But, in the second paragraph, I say zebra stripes are a popular pattern for furniture and decorations. I'll delete that detail since it doesn't relate to how stripes work in nature.

● **Elaboration** Do I give credit whenever I use a quotation or paraphrase something from a source? No, I don't. I paraphrased the explanation of *concealing coloration* from *Encyclopedia Britannica*. I'll add the phrase "According to *Encyclopedia Britannica*" to that sentence. Then I'll add the encyclopedia to the list of sources at the end of my chapter.

 **Guided Practice**

**Read the excerpt below from Bella's draft of the assignment. Then complete the activities. Use the Hints for help.**

### Bella's Draft

One purpose for animal communication is sharing information. For example, gazelles jump up and down to warn the herd when cheetahs are near. Bees dance to share where to find food. When sage grouse want to attract mates, they change their appearance dramatically and dance all night.

Another reason animals communicate is to defend their territory. Siamese fighting fish, for instance, make themselves look stronger and quicker than another fighting fish, but pet stores breed these fish for their beauty. They fight by extending their fins and beating their tails.

**1 Organization**  Identify the main idea of Bella's first paragraph. Do all the facts and details in that paragraph support this idea? Explain why or why not.

> **HINT** The main idea is often stated in the first sentence.

_____

_____

_____

**2 Elaboration**  Which detail in the second paragraph does not belong in Bella's draft? Explain your answer.

> **HINT** First, identify the topic of Bella's draft. Then find what doesn't belong.

_____

_____

> **HINT** What are two ways that writers can cite their sources?

**3 Elaboration**  How should Bella give credit for the facts she has taken from her sources?

_____

_____

**Turn and Talk**  Take turns reading aloud your body paragraphs. After each paragraph, stop and discuss. Do all the facts and details relate to the main idea?

### Write Time ✏

Use the Informational Writing Checklist passed out by your teacher to evaluate your draft for **Ideas**, **Organization**, and **Elaboration**.

# Step 7 Revise: Second Read

**W.5.2d:** Use . . . domain-specific vocabulary to inform about or explain the topic.

**L.5.6:** Acquire and use accurately grade-appropriate . . . domain-specific words and phrases. . . .

**FOCUS** Domain-Specific Vocabulary

In this step, you'll look for places to add **domain-specific vocabulary**. These words and phrases belong to a particular subject, or *domain,* such as science, and they help writers express ideas precisely when writing informational or explanatory texts. Using domain-specific words and terms—and explaining them clearly—will help your readers learn more about your topic.

When revising your writing for language, ask yourself: *Am I using correct, domain-specific words? Have I clearly explained any words my audience might not know?*

Here are some domain-specific words you might use in your book chapter about animal communication:

- **adaptation** – a change in a characteristic or behavior that helps a life-form survive
- **evolve** – to change over time in response to one's surroundings
- **habitat** – the natural home of an animal, plant, or other life-form
- **predator** – an animal that hunts and eats other animals
- **trait** – a feature or behavior that occurs naturally in a life-form

## Modeled Instruction

**Read the excerpt below from "Hiding in Plain Sight." Note how Caleb Lawrence used domain-specific words to make his ideas clear. Then complete the activities.**

**From MENTOR TEXT** *page 122*

For an animal in the wild, threats to survival are everywhere. All habitats have risks. For example, water sources can dry up. Food can grow scarce. The weather can turn dangerous without warning. But perhaps most worrisome to animals is the constant danger of becoming another animal's lunch. To avoid being eaten by hungry predators (or better yet, to stalk their own prey!), many animals use **camouflage**—the natural coloring or shape of their bodies which allows them to disappear into their surroundings. There are three main types of animal camouflage.

**1** How does Caleb help his readers understand the domain-specific term *camouflage*?

_____

_____

_____

**2** **Underline** another example of a domain-specific word. Then explain how Caleb makes its meaning clear to readers.

_____

_____

_____

Read the following paragraph from an early draft of the Mentor Text. Then use the Hints to complete the activities that follow.

**MENTOR TEXT Draft**

The third type of camouflage is **mimicry**. In mimicry, an animal copies the traits of an animal that a predator would not want to eat. For example, a hawk won't eat monarch butterflies because they are poisonous to birds. As a result, the viceroy butterfly has changed over a long period of time to look a lot like a monarch butterfly. Looking like a monarch butterfly is a useful change to a characteristic because it helps the viceroy not be eaten.

**3** The writer wants to add a definition to help a younger audience understand the domain-specific term *traits*. Which is the best definition for the writer to add? Circle the correct answer.

**A** changes to a life-form over time

**B** natural homes of life-forms

**C** animals that eat other animals

**D** natural features or behaviors

> **HINT** Replace the word *traits* in the draft with each definition. Which choice makes the most sense?

**4** Read these sentences from the draft of the Mentor Text:

As a result, the viceroy butterfly has <u>changed over a long period of time</u> to look a lot like a monarch butterfly. Looking like a monarch butterfly is a useful <u>change to a characteristic</u> because it helps the viceroy not be eaten.

Rewrite the sentences on the lines below, replacing the underlined words with the domain-specific terms that convey the meaning more precisely.

> **HINT** Use the list of terms and definitions on the opposite page to choose the best replacements.

_____

_____

_____

**Turn and Talk** Take turns reading aloud your drafts. Discuss how you can include definitions or other information to help your audience understand challenging science terms.

**Write Time** ✏️

Use the Informational Writing Checklist passed out by your teacher to evaluate your draft for **Language**.

# Step 8 Edit for Conventions

**W.5.5:** With guidance and support from peers and adults, develop and strengthen writing as needed by . . . editing.

**L.5.2b:** Use a comma to separate an introductory element from the rest of the sentence.

**FOCUS** Introductory Elements

The last step is to make sure that your spelling, grammar, and punctuation are correct. In this step, you'll focus on using a comma to separate an introductory element from the rest of the sentence.

- An **introductory element** is a word or phrase that comes at the beginning of a sentence. Introductory elements can include single words, prepositional phrases, and dependent clauses.

- Use a **comma (,)** to set off an introductory word or phrase from the rest of the sentence.

  **Yes,** many animals use camouflage.

  **With a little practice,** you can learn to spot them.

  **If you walk around your neighborhood,** you'll probably find some.

> **Language Handbook** To learn more about punctuating introductory elements, turn to page 198.

## Modeled Instruction

**Read the following excerpt from a draft of "Hiding in Plain Sight." Then complete the activities.**

**MENTOR TEXT** Draft

> The second type of camouflage is **disguise**. Like concealing coloration, disguise helps animals blend in with their surroundings. However disguised animals rely not just on coloration but also shape and texture. Most animals that use disguise are insects. For instance the walking leaf insect matches the shape, texture, and color of the plant leaves in its habitat. Because they live on tree trunks lantern flies are rough, scaly, and brown. As a last example certain tree frogs look like velvety lumps of green moss.

**1** In the second sentence, **underline** the introductory element, including the comma.

**2** The sentence with the wavy line is missing a comma. **Add** a comma in the proper place after the introductory element.

**3** Three other sentences in the draft need commas following their introductory elements. **Underline** each introductory element, and **add** a comma in the proper place after each one.

Read the following excerpt from an early draft of "Hiding in Plain Sight." Then complete the activities. Use the Hints for help.

---

**MENTOR TEXT  Draft**

The third type of camouflage is **mimicry**. If you know anything about monarch butterflies you might have heard that they are poisonous to birds. As a result dangerous predators like hawks won't eat monarch butterflies. Because of this fact the viceroy butterfly has grown to look a lot like a monarch butterfly.

---

**4** Read this sentence from the draft:

> If you know anything about monarch butterflies you might have heard that they are poisonous to birds.

**HINT** Identify the dependent clause, which has both a subject and a verb.

Which of the following should replace the underlined words to make the sentence correct? Circle the correct answer.

**A**  If, you know anything about monarch butterflies you might have heard

**B**  If you know, anything about monarch butterflies you might have heard

**C**  If you know anything, about monarch butterflies you might have heard

**D**  If you know anything about monarch butterflies, you might have heard

**5** The sentence below contains an error in punctuation. Underline the phrase that should be followed by a comma. Then add the comma.

As a result dangerous predators like hawks won't eat monarch butterflies.

**HINT** Imagine reading the sentence aloud. The comma goes where you pause briefly.

**6** The sentence below contains an error in punctuation. Underline the phrase that should be followed by a comma. Then add the comma.

Because of this fact the viceroy butterfly has evolved to look like a monarch butterfly.

**HINT** Which part of the sentence introduces the main clause?

**Turn and Talk** Read aloud your book chapters. Listen for any sentences that have introductory elements. Check that these elements have commas after them.

**Write Time** ✏

Use the Informational Writing Checklist passed out by your teacher to evaluate your draft for **Conventions**.

# Writing an Opinion: Speech

W.5.1: Write opinion pieces on topics or texts, supporting a point of view with reasons and information.

W.5.7: Conduct short research projects that use several sources to build knowledge through investigation of different aspects of a topic.

## Sharing Opinions

Alia's class has been talking about the way people communicate. Her teacher, Mr. Morgan, feels that e-mail has harmed the art of letter writing. He says letters are more thoughtful than e-mail because people have to consider what to say.

Alia disagrees. She tells Mr. Morgan there are many reasons an e-mail is better than a letter. "Prove it," Mr. Morgan says. "Write a speech giving your opinion and your reasons. Then you can present your speech to the class." Alia does just that. Part of her speech is shown on the tablet below.

Mr. Morgan listens carefully to Alia's speech. Then he sends her an e-mail saying, "You made some good points, Alia. Sometimes e-mail really is better!"

Speaking about your opinion is a good way to share it. Your listeners can hear how strongly you feel, and you might even get them to agree with you!

---

4:15 PM     90%

I have been using e-mail to keep in touch with my cousin Sherine, who lives in Egypt. I feel e-mail is a great way to communicate for many reasons.

First, e-mail gets to your friend quickly. You don't have to worry about whether it got lost, because you get a reply right away.

Second, you can easily attach pictures to an e-mail. Here's a picture Sherine sent me yesterday. The picture was taken . . .

# What Is Opinion Writing?

In opinion writing, a writer states an opinion that reflects his or her point of view—thoughts, feelings, or beliefs—about a topic. The writer supports this opinion by giving strong reasons and then using evidence, such as facts and details, to explain each reason.

## KEY FEATURES | Opinion Writing

- an introduction that gets readers interested in the topic and presents a clear opinion statement
- paragraphs that provide logically ordered reasons supported by evidence
- linking words, phrases, and clauses that clearly connect the opinion to reasons, and the reasons to evidence
- a conclusion that restates the opinion and leaves readers with something to think about

## Steps for Writing

On the following pages, you'll learn the steps for writing your own speech.

| | | | |
|---|---|---|---|
| **Step 1** | Study a Mentor Text | **Step 5** | Draft Your Speech |
| **Step 2** | Unpack Your Assignment | **Step 6** | Revise: First Read |
| **Step 3** | Find Text Evidence | **Step 7** | Revise: Second Read |
| **Step 4** | Organize Your Evidence | **Step 8** | Edit for Conventions |

The Research Path

# Step 1  Study a Mentor Text

FOCUS  Read as a Writer

Before you write your speech, you'll study a model. First, read to understand what it's about. Then reread to understand how it was written.

**As you reread the Mentor Text, do the numbered activities. They'll help you understand the key features of an opinion speech.**

**MENTOR TEXT: Speech**

## Is Texting Ruining Communication?
### by Marina Lopez

1    Has texting gone too far? I text as much as anyone and can't imagine not texting my friends when I want to meet. I know how easy it is to text. I know how much I like it, too. I can spend hours texting about nothing at all and have a great time! Take a step back, though, and what you'll find is that texting is changing the way we communicate with others. After reading what psychologists and other experts have to say about texting, I believe that it can make communication less effective. There are a number of reasons for this.

2    The first reason, according to many experts, is that texting is a shallow way to communicate. A text doesn't have many details or much more than the basics. Think about it. You usually put only a few words in a text. Consequently, you can't explain much and run into problems. For example, the person you text may misunderstand your tone and get angry or upset. Or, someone may end up in the wrong place at the wrong time because you didn't give enough information. Sometimes, good communication takes more information than a text can provide.

3    Second, communication experts also say that more information is communicated by a phone conversation than by a text. I agree. You may still be using a cell phone, but a quick back-and-forth is not the same as hearing someone's voice. A voice gives clues you can't get from a text. In a phone call, you can tell if your friends are happy or angry, and whether they're joking or being mean, by the sound of their voice. People can put "lol" or a smiley face in a text, but you can't tell how they really feel.

**1 Opinion Statement**  The writer formed her opinion after doing some research. **Draw a dashed line** beneath the sentence in the introduction that states her opinion.

**2 Reasons**  In paragraphs 2–6, the writer gives several reasons to support her opinion. **Underline** each reason.

**3 Evidence**  In paragraph 3, why does the writer include the term *communication experts*?

_____

_____

_____

4     Third, talking to someone in person gives even more information than just talking by phone. Psychologists say we learn what people really mean not just from their voices but also from their faces. Body language is important, too. For example, if a person twists his hands, he may be nervous. If another person taps her feet, she may be impatient. You can't learn these things from a text.

5     Another reason is that psychologists say we lose important social skills if all we do is text our friends. For example, one psychologist pointed out that it's easy for a kid to text the words, "I'm sorry," but it's a lot harder to look someone in the eye and say the same thing. Does that matter? Yes! It's much harder to admit you're wrong when you have to say so in person, but it means a lot more when you do. Kids need to learn how to interact face-to-face.

6     Finally, many experts, especially teachers, say texting makes it more difficult for kids to learn spelling and grammar. Specifically, using shortcuts such as "gr8" for "great" or "wbu" for "What about you?" is not helping us learn the language skills we'll need for high school.

7     For all these reasons, I have come to see the rise of texting as a problem for communication. Texting is fun and fast, and it's an easy way to stay in touch. But we shouldn't let it replace actual conversation. If we spend less time texting, we'll learn how to communicate more effectively with others.

**4 Evidence** In paragraph 4, **underline** the two examples the writer uses to support the point that body language helps people understand the true meaning of a message.

**5 Linking Words, Phrases & Clauses** In paragraphs 5 and 6, the writer varies the linking words that signal additional reasons from the first-second-third pattern in earlier paragraphs. **Draw a box** around the word she uses instead in each paragraph.

**6 Conclusion** In her conclusion, the writer leaves her readers with an idea to think about. **Draw a dashed line** under the sentence that does this. Explain what the writer wants readers to think about.

_____

_____

_____

_____

_____

W.5.4: Produce clear and coherent writing in which the development and organization are appropriate to task, purpose, and audience.

# Step 2 Unpack Your Assignment

Before you begin writing, read your assignment carefully to identify your task, purpose, and audience.

The **purpose** of an opinion speech is to state your opinion about a topic and try to convince your **audience** to agree with you. When you read your assignment, look carefully for details about who your listeners are, what background knowledge they have, and how they might feel about the topic.

## 👥 Modeled Instruction

Marina Lopez, who wrote "Is Texting Ruining Communication?" on pages 154–155, was given the assignment below. She read it carefully and marked up important details.

**Read Marina's assignment. Then read the points in her Think Aloud, which tell how she identified her task, purpose, and audience.**

### MARINA'S Assignment

Your language arts class is doing a unit on modern technology. You are assigned to give a speech on this topic: "Is Texting Ruining Communication?" In your speech, you will give your opinion about whether texting has reduced people's ability to communicate with each other effectively.

**In your speech:**

- State your opinion about whether texting has reduced people's ability to communicate effectively.

- Provide logically ordered reasons to support your opinion.

- Support your reasons with evidence from reliable sources.

### Think Aloud

- **Audience**  The words *language arts class* tell me my classmates and teacher will be my audience. My classmates are big fans of texting. If I take the opinion that texting is harmful, I'll need to give strong reasons to convince them!

- **Purpose**  My purpose is to share my opinion about whether texting has harmed people's communication skills. I hope to convince my audience to agree with me.

- **Task**  My task is to write a speech. The bullets tell me three things I need to do to write it well. First, I need to state my opinion. The second bullet says I need "logically ordered reasons." That means I should give my reasons in an order that makes sense, and might be more convincing to my audience. One way might be to put the strongest reason first. The word *evidence* in the third bullet reminds me to include facts and details from my sources to support my reasons.

Now it's your turn to write a speech. Read Your Assignment carefully.
Then complete the activities, using the Hints for help.

## Your Assignment ✏

A local youth center is hosting a public debate about online social networking sites. The debate focuses on this question: "Do social networking sites really improve people's lives?" Anyone in your community is invited to participate. You decide to give a speech that offers your opinion on this topic.

**To prepare to write your speech, you will read the following:**

- from "Staying in Touch—All the Time" *pages 162–163*
- Social Media: For Better or Worse? *pages 164–167*

**In your speech:**

- State your opinion about whether using social media sites improves people's lives or does more harm than good.
- Provide logically ordered reasons to support your opinion.
- Support your reasons with evidence from your sources.

*Hi, I'm Azul, and I'm also going to be doing this assignment.*

**1** **Audience  Draw a box** around the words that tell your audience. How will knowing your audience help you plan your speech?

_____

_____

> **HINT** What can you infer about your audience's views on the topic?

**2** **Purpose**  What is the purpose of your speech?

_____

_____

> **HINT** What kind of speech are you giving?

**3** **Task  Underline** the details that tell what your speech should include.

**Turn and Talk**  Discuss how writing an opinion speech is similar to other types of opinion writing, such as essays or blog posts. How is it different?

> **HINT** What are the key features of opinion writing?

# The Research Path
## Writing from Sources

Join me on the path to gather evidence from sources!

**Read as a Reader**

## Sources

### READ Your Sources

**Go to pages 162–167**

- from "Staying in Touch—All the Time"
- **Social Media: For Better or Worse?**

Find out what these sources are about and what you can learn from them.

**Reread as a Writer**

### REREAD Your Sources

**Return to pages 162–167**
Use your mark-up strategy to identify important details in the sources.

Close Reading

## REVIEW Your Assignment

**Return to page 157**
Reread your task to
identify the types
of information you
will need to include
in your speech.

## Text Evidence

### FIND Text Evidence

**Go to pages 160–161**
Learn how to mark
important details
so you can find
them quickly later on.

## THINK It Through

**Go to pages 168–169**
Complete the activities
to help you connect
the ideas in the sources
to your assignment.

### ORGANIZE Your Evidence

**Go to pages 170–171**
Use a chart to
group your reasons
and supporting
evidence so that
you're ready to write.

**Need More Information?**
Yes, see Write Time, page 169

**Begin Writing!**
Go to pages 172–173

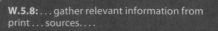

**W.5.8:** . . . gather relevant information from print . . . sources. . . .

# Step 3 Find Text Evidence

**FOCUS** Gather Information

You've unpacked your assignment and identified your task, purpose, and audience. Now you will look for information that will help you form your opinion and support it. To form an opinion, you need to first consider both sides of an issue. For this assignment, you should look for details that show how using social media *improves* people's lives and details showing how it is *harmful*.

Remember that details supporting an idea are often called **pros**. Details opposing an idea are called **cons**. As you reread the source texts, mark details showing how social media improves people's lives with a **P**, for *pro*. Mark details about the harmful effects with a **C**, for *con*. Then you'll be able to review the details easily when it's time to form your opinion.

## 👥 Modeled Instruction

To gather information for his speech, Azul underlined details and marked up the text as he read his source, "Social Media: For Better or Worse?"

**Read the text and Azul's Think Aloud to learn more about the reading and mark-up strategies he used.**

From **"Social Media"** *page 166*

Social media sites and apps can be used to educate people about pressing issues and can even change opinions. For example, <u>teens have been</u>   P <u>turning to social media as a way to learn about causes, from joining a community cleanup to fighting bullying</u>. . . .

Opponents of social media caution that it can result in behaviors that are problematic. <u>People</u>   C <u>frequently feel constant pressure to "keep up" by posting nonstop</u>. This can lead to stress and loneliness.

### Think Aloud

● The first paragraph says one use of social media is to "educate people." The second sentence gives examples of this—teens learning about and working for good causes. This definitely shows how social media can improve lives. I'll underline these details and mark them with a P.

● The next paragraph mentions "opponents of social media" and "problematic" behavior. That tells me the details will show some harmful effects of social media. One sentence gives an example of people feeling "pressure." This is a harmful effect, so I'll underline it and label it with a C.

## 👥 Guided Practice

**Read the following excerpt from "Social Media" and note the underlined detail. Then complete the activities, using the Hints for help.**

> From **"Social Media"** *page 166*
>
> C  For example, a condition known as social media anxiety disorder is a sign of trouble. Experts say that it comes about when people get addicted to social media. It can affect adults and young people, too. Some get upset when they compare themselves to others in their network. They may feel that they're not as accomplished or as popular as others. In 2012, researchers in the United Kingdom led a small study about the effects of social media. More than half of the participants said that social media sites had a negative impact. Two-thirds said that they had trouble relaxing and sleeping after using social media.

**1** Why is the underlined sentence marked with a C?

_____

_____

_____

> **HINT** Remember that C means "con." Look for words that suggest something negative.

**2** **Underline** two statements that describe how social media can affect people's feelings. **Mark** them with a P or C.

> **HINT** Look for words that describe feelings, either positive or negative.

**3** Reread the last two sentences in the excerpt. Would you mark them with a P or a C? Explain your answer.

> **HINT** What were the results of the study described in the excerpt?

_____

_____

💬 **Turn and Talk** Discuss how marking the pros and cons of using social media will help you form your opinion and find details to support it.

# from Staying in Touch— All the Time

**by Laurie Shinbaum,** *Appleseeds*

1   Do you like being poked?

2   Most people don't—unless it's on Facebook, a popular Internet site. Facebook members can poke a friend, which is a message that loosely means, "Hey, I'm still here!"

3   Not that long ago, Facebook did not exist. Today, social networking sites like Facebook make staying in touch easier than ever.

4   You know what a network is—a set of links or ties between one place, person, or thing and another. What about social? Social means having to do with groups of people, or society. So a social network is a set of links among people. Sometimes these sites are also called "social media."

5   Social networking sites like Facebook, Twitter, Ning, and MySpace are websites that connect people on the Internet. Through them, people are able to meet, speak, and share information with each other. These sites create virtual communities for adults—and sometimes teenagers. Today, we use the word *virtual* to mean something that exists but not in actual form. For example, Facebook creates a real community, but it is not a physical community like your town.

6    Facebook is one of the most popular social networking sites. It was created on a college campus in 2004. At first, it was open only to college students. Now you can join Facebook if you are over 13. (Between 13 and 18, you must be a high school or college student.) More than 500 million people around the world have joined.

7    Twitter is another hugely successful network. On Twitter people send short messages called "tweets" to and from cell phones and computers. A tweet can be no longer than 140 characters.

8    Schools use social networking, too. In some schools, teachers use special online networks to communicate with their students. They can give quizzes, assign homework, and send reminders about upcoming class work.

9    The social networks are improving every day. Who knows what social networks will exist for you in the future? You might even invent one of your own!

## Social Media Update

Since this article was first published in 2011, the social media landscape has shifted. Some teens have found new virtual hangouts, including the following:

**Instagram** Users post photos or short videos with captions, which their followers may "like" or comment on. A single post can get hundreds of responses.

**Snapchat** This app lets friends exchange photos or videos, and then the post disappears. But anyone can take a screenshot, so it's not really gone forever!

**Tumblr** On this site, users combine short messages with photos and videos to make super-short blogs.

**Google+** Users can watch their circles of friends grow on this networking site. A bonus is the chance to video-chat in Google Hangouts.

**Kik** This app is like texting, but it allows users to socialize as they send messages to each other.

# SOCIAL MEDIA
## For Better or Worse?

by Skye Najar

1    Though Ciara and Tomás are sitting right across from one another, the two friends stare at their phones, posting updates about the day's events. They talk for a few minutes as they eagerly wait for virtual responses. Then they turn back to their screens.

2    Does this scene sound familiar to you? If it doesn't yet, it might soon. Social media— digital communication such as texts, tweets, blogs, networking sites, and social apps—are everywhere. Connecting through social media has become the main way that many people interact with friends, family, and the world.

3    Is this constant use of social media a good thing or a bad thing? Opinions run strong on both sides of the issue. Let's start with the upside.

# Building Better Relationships

4      Advocates say that social media provide benefits that face-to-face communication alone can't offer. They enable connections to far more people and at greater speeds than any other type of communication. Users can find others who share their interests or face similar issues. Online interactions can be empowering. People make new friends who treasure the same books they do. They may take pride in the praise they get for posting "selfies," or photos they've taken of themselves.

5      Common Sense Media, a group focused on youth interactions with media, polled more than 1,000 teens ages 13 to 17. The survey found that 28% said they felt more outgoing because of social networking. Comparatively, only 5% said they felt less outgoing, and the rest of those in the survey said that social media had no effect on them.  The survey also found that more than half of the teens (52%) reported better relationships with friends as a result of social media. Only 4% said that it had a negative effect on their friendships.

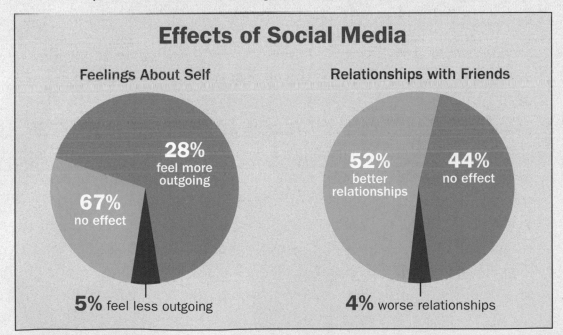

**Effects of Social Media**

Feelings About Self

**28%** feel more outgoing

**67%** no effect

**5%** feel less outgoing

Relationships with Friends

**52%** better relationships

**44%** no effect

**4%** worse relationships

6      There are educational advantages to social media, too.  Teachers can use social networking to share ideas for their classrooms. Students can use links to resources, such as videos and online lessons. They can also discuss school subjects in safe online communities. According to a 2007 study, at least 50% of American students with Internet access report using social media for educational purposes.

# Voting and Viewpoints

7      Social media can also serve as a way for voices to be heard. Presidential elections provide a good example of this kind of communication. In 2008, more than 25% of US voters under age 30 said they learned about the candidates' campaigns from social media. In 2012, voters could visit the candidates' profiles online and follow them to stay up-to-date with the news. A post-election tweet even set a record for the number of times it was re-tweeted.

8      Social media sites and apps can be used to educate people about pressing issues and can even change opinions. For example, teens have been turning to social media as a way to learn about causes, from joining a community cleanup to fighting bullying. Through their posts, teens can express their views and take action. A hashtag—a hash sign (#) followed by a word or phrase, added to a post—is one way to spread the word about an issue. It also helps teens find friends who think the way they do.

# Unhealthy Habits

9      Opponents of social media caution that it can result in behaviors that are problematic. People frequently feel constant pressure to "keep up" by posting nonstop. This can lead to stress and loneliness.

10      For example, a condition known as social media anxiety disorder is a sign of trouble. Experts say that it comes about when people get addicted to social media. It can affect adults and young people, too. Some get upset when they compare themselves to others in their network. They may feel that they're not as accomplished or as popular as others. In 2012, researchers in the United Kingdom led a small study about the effects of social media. More than half of the participants said that social media sites had a negative impact. Two-thirds said that they had trouble relaxing and sleeping after using social media.

11      Another habit that's becoming common is using virtual connections to replace real-life encounters. Parents worry that their teens don't know how to interact well with family and friends because they're so accustomed to digital contact. They worry, too, that teens may become less physically active and sleep less when hooked on social media. These behaviors can lead to health issues for some teens.

## A Tough Balancing Act

12    Social media can forge friendships but can also sour relationships between peers. In person, people tend to be more private and more careful about their words than when they're interacting virtually. Social media may cause misunderstandings and result in negative interactions. Some teens and kids say cruel things and mistreat others online in ways that they wouldn't face-to-face. Cyberbullying is one extreme result. A person or group may threaten another, making the victim feel miserable.

13    Finally, social media cause people to have trouble balancing schoolwork with virtual activity. A 2011 study found that college students who spent an average amount of time on social media were unaffected in their academics. The most frequent social media users, however, had lower grades. Students who used social media while studying also got lower test scores than their less distracted classmates.

It can be tempting to use social media while studying. But this can result in lower grades and test scores.

## Finding Our Way

14    With the ever-changing world of social media, we're coming to new understandings of what's normal and what's okay. Not that long ago, it would have been strange to broadcast to the world little things we've done on a typical day. Today, it's commonplace. Most experts agree that it's important to think carefully before engaging in social media. However, it can be a valuable tool when users reflect on what they're saying in updates and comments, as well as what images they're sharing.

15    Clearly, there is both good and harm that can come from social media. From day to day, opinions change. In the long run, though, it's up to us to decide how to use social media to our advantage.

**W.5.9b:** Apply *grade 5 Reading standards* to informational texts.

## Think It Through

**Use details from both sources to complete the following activities. Your answers will help you write your speech.**

**1** Based on the information you've read, do you think the use of social media improves people's lives or does more harm than good? Write your opinion statement below.

> **HINT** Look for sentences in both sources that you marked with a P.

_____

**2** List three reasons supporting your opinion about social media. The example below shows how you can combine related details into a single reason.

> **HINT** Use the notes and marks you made on the sources to help you develop your reasons.

**Example:**

Detail: Social media may cause misunderstandings between people.

Detail: Some kids say mean things and bully others online.

Reason: Using social media harms relationships.

Reason: _____

_____

Reason: _____

_____

Reason: _____

_____

**3** On the lines below, write an opinion statement that is **opposite** to the one you wrote for the first activity.

_____

**4** List three reasons that support the opinion statement you wrote in activity 3. Look back at the example in activity 2 to show how you can combine related details into a single reason.

**HINT** Look back at the details you marked with a P or C for ideas that support the other side.

Reason: _____

_____

Reason: _____

_____

Reason: _____

_____

**5** Now that you have completed activities 3 and 4, do you still hold the opinion you wrote in activity 1? Or has your opinion changed? Explain your answer.

**HINT** Which opinion seems best supported by the reasons you listed?

_____

_____

**6** Complete the frame below to express your opinion and reasons in one paragraph.

**HINT** Use your responses to activities 1 and 2 (or activities 3 and 4) to help you complete the frame.

I believe that social media sites _____

because [reason 1] _____ ,

[reason 2] _____ ,

and [reason 3] _____ .

**Write Time** 🖊

Return to your sources to find facts and details that support the three reasons you identified. Mark evidence for each reason with the code R-1, R-2, or R-3.

**W.5.5:** With guidance and support from peers and adults, develop and strengthen writing as needed by planning. . . .

**W.5.8:** . . . summarize or paraphrase information in notes. . . .

# Step 4  Organize Your Evidence

**FOCUS** Plan Your Speech

Now that you've formed your opinion, decided on your reasons, and gathered supporting evidence, it's time to organize your information.

Remember that each reason helps explain why listeners should agree with your opinion. In the same way, evidence, or the facts and details you marked in your sources, helps explain each reason. As you write your speech, each reason and its supporting evidence will make up one paragraph.

## Modeled Instruction

To organize his information, Azul created the chart below.

**Look at the underlined sentences from "Social Media." Notice how Azul used that information in his chart. Underline another detail that suports Azul's reason, and add it to the chart.**

From **"Social Media"** *page 165*

Advocates say that social media provide benefits that face-to-face communication alone can't offer. They enable connections to far more people and at greater speeds than any other type of communication. Users can find others who share their interests or face similar issues. Online interactions can be empowering. People make new friends who treasure the same books they do. They may take pride in the praise they get for posting "selfies," or photos they've taken of themselves.

**Azul's Chart**

| Opinion: Using social media improves people's lives. | |
|---|---|
| **Reason 1** Social networks allow fast, easy communication among people all over the world. | **Evidence** • People can find others who share their interests or problems.  • _____ |

## Guided Practice

**Azul's classmate Luna has the opposite opinion. Help her continue filling out her chart by completing the activities. Use the Hints for help.**

From **"Social Media"** *page 167*

    Social media can forge friendships but can also sour relationships between peers. In person, people tend to be more private and more careful about their words than when they're interacting virtually. Social media <u>may cause</u> <u>misunderstandings</u> and result in negative interactions. Some teens and kids say cruel things and mistreat others online in ways that they wouldn't face-to-face. Cyberbullying is one extreme result. A person or group may threaten another, making the victim feel miserable.

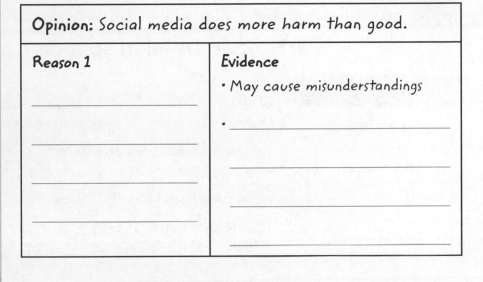

**Luna's Chart**

| Opinion: Social media does more harm than good. | |
|---|---|
| **Reason 1** | **Evidence**<br>• May cause misunderstandings<br><br>• _____ |

1. Read the excerpt carefully. What reason do all of the details in this excerpt support? Write the reason in Luna's chart.

> **HINT** How can social media affect relationships?

2. Identify another detail that Luna could use as evidence to support this reason. **Underline** the detail and add it to the chart in your own words.

> **HINT** How can social media influence the way people behave?

3. What example from the excerpt should Luna be sure to include as evidence in her speech? Explain your answer.

_____

_____

> **HINT** What is a particularly important issue among teens and kids?

**Turn and Talk**   Discuss the difference between reasons and evidence. Why is it important to support your reasons with evidence?

**Write Time** 🖉

In your own chart, record the reasons for your opinion and then organize the evidence you identified to support each reason.

# Step 5 Draft Your Speech

W.5.1: Write opinion pieces on topics or texts, supporting a point of view with reasons and information.

W.5.1a: Introduce a topic or text clearly, state an opinion, and create an organizational structure in which ideas are logically grouped to support the writer's purpose.

**FOCUS** Write an Introduction

Read this chart to learn more about the main parts of an opinion speech. You can refer back to this information for help as you write your draft.

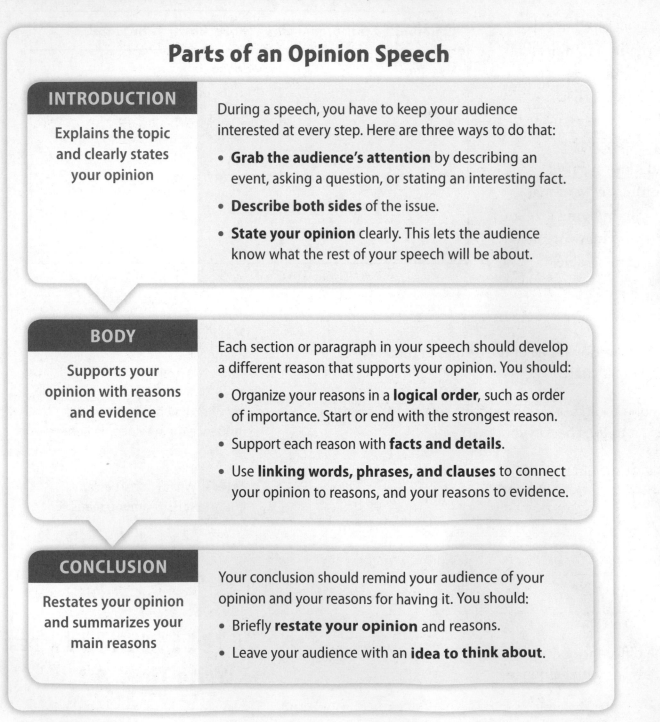

## Parts of an Opinion Speech

**INTRODUCTION**

Explains the topic and clearly states your opinion

During a speech, you have to keep your audience interested at every step. Here are three ways to do that:

- **Grab the audience's attention** by describing an event, asking a question, or stating an interesting fact.
- **Describe both sides** of the issue.
- **State your opinion** clearly. This lets the audience know what the rest of your speech will be about.

**BODY**

Supports your opinion with reasons and evidence

Each section or paragraph in your speech should develop a different reason that supports your opinion. You should:

- Organize your reasons in a **logical order**, such as order of importance. Start or end with the strongest reason.
- Support each reason with **facts and details**.
- Use **linking words, phrases, and clauses** to connect your opinion to reasons, and your reasons to evidence.

**CONCLUSION**

Restates your opinion and summarizes your main reasons

Your conclusion should remind your audience of your opinion and your reasons for having it. You should:

- Briefly **restate your opinion** and reasons.
- Leave your audience with an **idea to think about**.

# Draft Your INTRODUCTION

Practice writing the parts of an introduction. Study each sample text below.
Then try writing each part of your own introduction.

INTRODUCTION

BODY

CONCLUSION

## Grab the Audience's Attention

| Sample Text | Parents, teachers, and other grown-ups often say kids spend too much time texting. No kid wants to hear that—especially when we're in the middle of texting! |
|---|---|
| Your Speech | |

**HINT** What fact is probably true of most readers' social media habits?

## Describe Both Sides of the Issue

| Sample Text | On the one hand, texting allows people to communicate quickly and easily. But texting is changing the way we communicate with others, and many of these changes are not for the best. |
|---|---|
| Your Speech | |

**HINT** Why is social media important to many people? Why do others object to it?

## State Your Opinion

| Sample Text | In many ways, texting is far less effective than ordinary conversation. |
|---|---|
| Your Speech | |

**HINT** How do you feel about social media? State your opinion here.

**Turn and Talk** Discuss why clearly explaining both sides of an issue is important when sharing your own opinion.

## Write Time

Use your ideas from this page to draft your introduction. Then begin drafting your body paragraphs.

**W.5.1b:** Provide logically ordered reasons that are supported by facts and details.
**W.5.8:** ... paraphrase information in ... finished work....

FOCUS  Paraphrasing Information

## Draft Your BODY

As you draft your body paragraphs, you will give reasons for your opinion that are supported by evidence. Sometimes, you will **quote** evidence directly from your sources. Other times, you will **paraphrase** it, or express it in your own words.

Writers paraphrase information to share it in a shorter way than the original or to change the wording so it's more appropriate for their audience. They also want to avoid **plagiarizing**, which means using the exact words of a text without using quotation marks or giving credit to the source. When paraphrasing:

- Combine related details into a statement that captures the idea they share.

- Keep the important ideas, but change the wording to your own.

INTRODUCTION

BODY

CONCLUSION

## Modeled Instruction

**Read the excerpt from a source Marina used to write her speech. Then read the Think Aloud to see how she decided to paraphrase details from the source.**

**From "Texting Is Not Nearly Enough"**

Texting communicates information, but remember what it can't communicate. In addition to voices and facial expressions, texting cannot communicate body language. Studies have shown that when people are nervous, fearful, or anxious, they tend to twist their hands. The same studies have shown that people often express impatience by tapping their feet. Finally, when people feel insecure, threatened, or angry, they might cross their arms in front of their bodies. When it comes to understanding what people are saying, their body language is as important as their words.

**Think Aloud**

● This paragraph gives examples of how texting can't convey body language. These examples support my opinion that texting isn't always an effective way to communicate, so I'll include them in my speech.

● Including *all* these examples will take up too much of my speech. And I can't quote all these examples. If I do, the speech won't sound like me anymore. So, I'll paraphrase the examples and write, "If a person twists his hands, he may be nervous. If another person taps her feet, she may be impatient." That sounds good: I've given the examples in my own voice and in a way that's easy for the audience to follow.

● The last sentence expresses an idea I strongly believe—that body language can say as much as words. In fact, I can't say it any better than that. Also, I want to show my audience that I've read this author and agree with her ideas. For these reasons, I might directly quote this sentence. Of course, I'll be sure to use quotation marks and give credit to the author.

Read the following excerpt from "Social Media." Then complete the activities, using the Hints for help.

From **"Social Media"** *page 165*

Common Sense Media, a group focused on youth interactions with media, polled more than 1,000 teens ages 13 to 17. The survey found that 28% said they felt more outgoing because of social networking. Comparatively, only 5% said they felt less outgoing, and the rest of those in the survey said that social media had no effect on them. The survey also found that more than half of the teens (52%) reported better relationships with friends as a result of social media. Only 4% said that it had a negative effect on their friendships.

**Azul's Draft**

Social media can help people feel more confident. A survey by Common Sense Media shows that social media make some teens feel "more outgoing." Only 5% said they felt less outgoing. The survey also found that 52% reported better relationships with their friends because of social media.

**1** Read the underlined sentences in Azul's draft. Explain why these sentences are not a good example of paraphrasing.

_____

_____

> **HINT** Compare Azul's wording to the source. How well does he put the information into his own words?

**2** On the lines below, rewrite the underlined section of Azul's draft to correctly paraphrase the ideas from his source.

_____

_____

> **HINT** How could the ideas in the sentences be combined and simplified?

> **HINT** Is there anything special about the way the information is conveyed in the source?

**3** Read the underlined sentence in "Social Media." Should Azul paraphrase this sentence or use it as a quotation? Explain your answer.

_____

_____

**Write Time** ✏️

Finish drafting the body of your speech. Then draft a conclusion using the tips from the chart on page 172 for help.

**Turn and Talk** Practice paraphrasing small sections of your source texts. Give your partner feedback about whether the wording is too close to the original.

# Step 6 Revise: First Read

**W.5.4:** Produce clear and coherent writing in which the development and organization are appropriate to task, purpose, and audience.

**W.5.5:** With guidance and support from peers and adults, develop and strengthen writing as needed by . . . revising. . . .

**FOCUS** Organization and Elaboration

As you revise your speech, use your Opinion Writing Checklist to check your writing. Work through the checklist, one line at a time. Reread the related parts of your speech to decide whether you did your best possible work for each trait described. In this step, you will check your speech for three of the traits in the categories of Organization and Elaboration.

## Modeled Instruction

The Mentor Text writer, Marina Lopez, used the same checklist to evaluate her draft.

**Read her Think Aloud to see how she checked her speech.**

### MENTOR TEXT  Draft

Another problem with texting is that we lose important social skills if we only text our friends. It's easy to text the words "I'm sorry," but it's harder to look someone in the eye and say the same thing. Does that matter? Yes! It's much harder to admit you're wrong when you have to say so in person, but it means a lot more when you do. Body language is an important type of information you can't get through texting. For example, people twisting their hands or tapping their feet may be nervous. Kids need to learn how to interact face to face.

Finally, many experts say texting makes it more difficult for kids to learn spelling and grammar.

I have come to see the rise of texting as a problem for communication. Texting is fun and fast, and it's an easy way to stay in touch. But we shouldn't let it replace actual conversation. If we spend less time texting, we'll learn how to communicate better with others.

### Think Aloud

● **Organization**  Do I group each reason with related facts, details, and examples? The first paragraph is confusing. It begins by talking about the loss of social skills, but then it talks about body language. The examples about body language don't belong in this paragraph. I'll draft a new paragraph that talks about how some information, such as body language, can't be understood through texting.

● **Elaboration**  Do I provide enough examples to support my reasons? My paragraph about spelling and grammar is a bit vague. It needs some specific examples of how texting can make it difficult to learn proper spelling and grammar. I'll add examples of texting shortcuts, such as "gr8" for "great" or "wbu" for "What about you?"

● **Organization**  Does my conclusion connect back to my reasons? It doesn't. I just restate my opinion and admit that texting has some good points. But I have so many reasons that restating them would make my conclusion too long. I'll add the linking phrase "For all these reasons" to the start of the paragraph. That phrase reminds my listeners that I've given several reasons.

Read the excerpt below from Azul's draft of the assignment. Then complete the activities. Use the Hints for help.

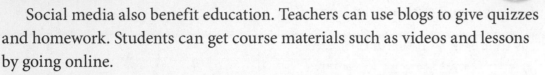

### Azul's Draft

Social media also benefit education. Teachers can use blogs to give quizzes and homework. Students can get course materials such as videos and lessons by going online.

News can also spread quickly through social media. Most people now get news from social networks. They still use them for personal messages, though.

I feel that social networks do improve people's lives. As these sites grow, they will break more barriers between people around the world.

**1 Organization** Azul has included an unrelated detail with one of his reasons. **Cross out** the detail in the draft, and then explain why it doesn't belong here.

> **HINT** Each sentence in a paragraph should be connected to the main idea.

_____

_____

**2 Elaboration** Has Azul provided enough details to support his reasons? Explain your answer. If he has not, suggest a detail he could add to the draft.

> **HINT** Look at the details you marked in your sources to find facts that could be added.

_____

_____

_____

**3 Organization** Evaluate Azul's conclusion. How could he improve it?

> **HINT** Does Azul's conclusion connect to his reasons?

_____

_____

_____

**Turn and Talk** Read your body paragraphs aloud. Listen for reasons that are not supported with enough facts, details, and examples.

### Write Time ✏

Use the Opinion Writing Checklist passed out by your teacher to evaluate your draft for **Ideas**, **Organization**, and **Elaboration**.

# Step 7 Revise: Second Read

**W.5.5:** With guidance and support from peers and adults . . . develop and strengthen writing as needed by . . . revising. . . .

**L.5.3a:** Expand, combine, and reduce sentences for meaning, reader/listener interest, and style.

**FOCUS** Sentence Variety

You've drafted and revised your ideas. Now it's time to make sure your ideas flow smoothly. You can do this by varying sentence lengths so there is a mix of long and short sentences. Using sentence variety helps to keep your audience interested.

- You can **expand** a sentence by adding details that make it more informative.

| Draft Sentence | My friends love to text. |
|---|---|
| Final Sentence | My friends love the abbreviations and symbols of texting. |

- You can **shorten** a sentence by deleting unnecessary words.

| Draft Sentence | I, on the other hand, neither enjoy, like, nor love texting. |
|---|---|
| Final Sentence | I, on the other hand, do not enjoy texting. |

- You can **combine** short sentences with related ideas into longer ones.

| Draft Sentences | I like texting with my friends. Still, I'd rather phone them. |
|---|---|
| Final Sentence | Although I like texting with my friends, I'd rather phone them. |

**Language Handbook** To learn more about sentence variety, turn to pages 206 and 208.

## Modeled Instruction

**Read the following excerpt from a draft of "Is Texting Ruining Communication?" Then complete the activities.**

### MENTOR TEXT Draft

Many experts say that texting is a shallow way to communicate. A text doesn't have many details, examples, facts, features, or points beyond the basics. Think about it. You usually put only a few words in a text. Consequently, you can't explain much and run into problems. For example, the person you text may misunderstand your tone. As a result, he or she might become angry or upset.

**1** On the lines below, write a shortened version of the first underlined sentence.

_____

_____

**2** On the lines below, combine the second and third underlined sentences into one longer sentence.

_____

_____

Read the following paragraph from an early draft of the Mentor Text. Then use the Hints to complete the activities that follow.

**MENTOR TEXT** Draft

Expressing emotion in texts is challenging. People find ways to do it. We can write "lol," we can make smiley faces, and we can even insert funny or sad pictures. But phone calls are still better. In a phone call, you can tell how your friend feels.

**3** Read the following sentences from the draft:

Expressing emotion in texts is challenging. People find ways to do it.

On the lines below, combine this pair of sentences.

**HINT** What are some words you can use to combine sentences?

_____

_____

**4** Read the following sentence from the draft:

We can write "lol," we can make smiley faces, and we can even insert funny or sad pictures.

**HINT** Look for a phrase that is repetitive.

Which of the following best shortens the sentence? Circle the correct answer.

**A** We can write "lol," smiley faces, and funny or sad pictures.

**B** We can write "lol," can make smiley faces, even insert funny or sad pictures.

**C** We can write "lol," make smiley faces, and even insert funny or sad pictures.

**D** We can write "lol," we can make smiley faces, insert funny or sad pictures.

**5** Read this sentence from the draft:

In a phone call, you can tell how your friends feel.

**HINT** What are some words that describe how a person might feel?

Revise the sentence, adding details so it is more interesting to read.

_____

_____

**Turn and Talk** Take turns reading your speeches aloud. Point out where your partner could add variety by expanding, shortening, or combining sentences.

**Write Time** 🖉

Use the Opinion Writing Checklist passed out by your teacher to evaluate your draft for **Language**.

# Step 8 Edit for Conventions

**W.5.5:** With guidance and support from peers and adults, develop and strengthen writing as needed by . . . editing.

**L.5.1b:** Form and use the perfect (e.g., *I had walked; I have walked; I will have walked*) verb tenses.

**FOCUS** Perfect Verb Tenses

The last step is to make sure that your spelling, punctuation, and grammar are correct. In this step, you'll focus on forming **perfect verb tenses**, which tell about actions that happened, that will happen, or that may happen again.

Perfect verb tenses are made by joining a form of the helping verb *have* with the **past participle form** of a main verb. The chart below shows some examples of perfect verb tenses.

| Tense | Description | Example |
|---|---|---|
| **Present perfect** | an action that began in the past and may happen again | My father **has written** thousands of e-mails. |
| **Past perfect** | an action that was completed before a certain past moment | Before e-mail, he **had written** his letters by hand. |
| **Future perfect** | an action that will be completed before a certain future time | By next year, he **will have written** his ten thousandth e-mail. |

**Language Handbook** To learn more about perfect verb tenses, turn to page 265.

## Modeled Instruction

**Read the following excerpt from a draft of "Is Texting Ruining Communication?" Then complete the activities.**

**MENTOR TEXT  Draft**

Experts say texting had made it harder for kids to learn spelling and grammar. Shortcuts like "gr8" will not have gave us the language skills we need.

That is why people who text all the time have went too far. For them, texting became an actual problem. It may be fun, fast, and easy. But we shouldn't let it replace talking. If all we do is text, we will lost an important way to communicate.

**1** The verb phrase in the first sentence contains a verb tense error. **Cross out** the incorrect verb and **write** the correct verb above it.

**2** The verb phrase in the second sentence contains a verb tense error. On the line below, rewrite the phrase to correct the error.

_____

**3** There are three more errors using perfect tense in the draft. **Cross out** incorrect verbs and **write** correct verbs above them.

## 👥 Guided Practice

**Read the following excerpt from an early draft of "Is Texting Ruining Communication?" Then complete the activities. Use the Hints for help.**

> **MENTOR TEXT** Draft
>
> A text doesn't have many details, which leads to confusion. You probably seen this problem for yourself. Think about a time when you were texting with a friend who suddenly got angry. Your friend have misunderstood your tone or something you said. Or imagine that your friend texts you directions. You will have went to the wrong place before you realized she made a mistake. Sometimes a text just can't provide enough information.

**4** Read this sentence from the speech:

> You probably <u>seen</u> this problem for yourself.

How should the underlined part be corrected? Circle the correct answer.

**A** had seen

**B** has seen

**C** have seen

**D** have saw

> **HINT** The sentence suggests an action that began in the past and may continue to happen.

**5** Read this sentence from the speech:

> Your friend <u>have misunderstood</u> your tone or something you said.

Circle the word that makes the underlined phrase incorrect. Then write a corrected sentence on the line that follows.

> **HINT** When did the friend misunderstand? Was it before the moment when the friend got angry?

**6** Read this sentence from the speech:

> You <u>will have went</u> to the wrong place before you realized she made a mistake.

Write the corrected verb phrase on the line that follows.

> **HINT** Which action will be completed before the other?

**Turn and Talk** Take turns reading your speeches aloud. Discuss whether you are using perfect verb tenses correctly.

### Write Time ✏️

Use the Opinion Writing Checklist passed out by your teacher to evaluate your draft for **Conventions**.

# Language Handbook

## Table of Contents

## Lesson 1
# Coordinating and Subordinating Conjunctions

**L.5.1a:** Explain the function of conjunctions ... in general and their function in particular sentences.

**Introduction** A **conjunction** is a word used to connect words, phrases, or clauses.

- **Coordinating conjunctions** connect words, phrases, or clauses of equal importance.

| Coordinating | When to Use | Example |
|---|---|---|
| and | to add information | Many animals live in places with plenty of food and water. |
| but | to show a difference | Deer eat many plants but still do not always get enough food. |
| or | to show a choice | They know that finding food is a matter of life or death. |
| so | to show cause and effect | They need more food, so they move on in search of it. |

- **Subordinating conjunctions** are used to connect a **dependent clause** to another clause. A dependent clause has a subject and a predicate but cannot stand alone.

| Subordinating | When to Use | Example |
|---|---|---|
| because | to explain why | Raccoons don't mind living in populated areas because they aren't afraid of people. |
| before, during, when, while | to show time | When deer cannot find food in their natural habitats, they will often go looking for it in people's yards. |
| although, unless | to show contrast | Although some animals avoid living near humans, other animals are comfortable being near people. |

**Guided Practice** Write a conjunction from the box to complete each sentence.

**HINT** If you're not certain which conjunction to use in a sentence, try each one.

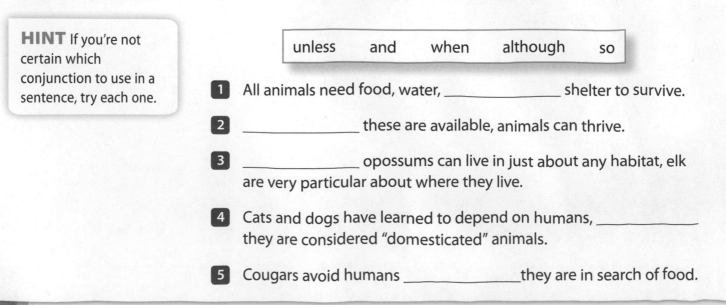

| unless | and | when | although | so |

**1** All animals need food, water, _____ shelter to survive.

**2** _____ these are available, animals can thrive.

**3** _____ opossums can live in just about any habitat, elk are very particular about where they live.

**4** Cats and dogs have learned to depend on humans, _____ they are considered "domesticated" animals.

**5** Cougars avoid humans _____ they are in search of food.

## Independent Practice

**For numbers 1–5, choose the best conjunction to complete each sentence.**

1. Farming, construction, _____ other human activities are affecting wild tigers in Asia.

   A but

   B so

   C and

   D or

2. Many groups are working to protect the tiger, _____ studies show that the animals have lost a great deal of their habitat.

   A but

   B so

   C and

   D or

3. _____ habitat loss is a big problem for tigers, it is not the only danger they face.

   A Since

   B Because

   C Before

   D Although

4. Tigers in some areas are destroyed _____ poachers kill them for their skins.

   A during

   B because

   C although

   D before

5. _____ governments take action, these animals will remain in danger.

   A Because

   B During

   C Although

   D Unless

## Lesson 2
# Prepositions and Prepositional Phrases

**L.5.1a:** Explain the function of . . . prepositions . . . in general and their function in particular sentences.

**Introduction**    A **preposition** is a word that shows how other words in a sentence are related. Words such as *about, by, in, of, on, to,* and *under* are prepositions.

- A **prepositional phrase** begins with a preposition and ends with a noun or a pronoun. The noun or pronoun is called the **object** of the preposition.

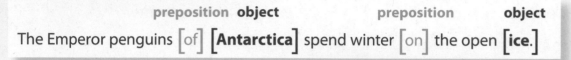

preposition **object**      preposition      **object**

The Emperor penguins [of] [**Antarctica**] spend winter [on] the open [**ice.**]

- A preposition tells about the relationship between the object of the preposition and another word in the sentence. Look at these sentences.

> Emperor penguins swim **under the** ice when they hunt.
>
> I recently saw a movie **about these amazing** penguins.

- In the first sentence, the preposition *under* tells about the relationship between *ice* and the verb *swim*. In the second sentence, the preposition *about* tells about the relationship between *penguins* and the noun *movie*.

- A prepositional phrase sometimes tells *how, when, where,* or *what kind*. In the sentences you just read, the prepositional phrase *under the ice* tells *where* the penguins swim. The prepositional phrase *about these amazing penguins* tells *what kind* of movie it was.

**Guided Practice**    **Underline the prepositional phrase in each sentence and circle the preposition. Then draw an arrow from the object of the preposition to the word it relates to.**

**HINT** Most prepositional phrases come after the noun or verb they describe.

**Example:**
I read a <u>book</u> **about Emperor penguins.**

1. Emperor penguins breed in the winter.

2. Female Emperor penguins lay eggs on the ice.

3. Males watch the eggs while the females travel to the sea.

4. The warmth of the males' feathers protects the eggs.

5. The females return and provide food for the little chicks.

### 👤 Independent Practice

**For numbers 1–3, choose the prepositional phrase in each sentence.**

**1** Emperor penguins can be found on only one continent.

   **A** found on only one continent

   **B** can be found

   **C** only one continent

   **D** on only one continent

**2** Antarctica's winter begins in late March.

   **A** winter begins

   **B** begins in

   **C** in late March

   **D** begins in late March

**3** There are 17 types of penguins, and the Emperor penguin is the largest.

   **A** of penguins

   **B** and the Emperor penguin

   **C** is the largest

   **D** are 17 types of

**For numbers 4 and 5, answer the question.**

**4** Read this sentence.

   > Most animals move <u>to</u> a warmer place each winter, but Emperor penguins do not.

   What is the purpose of the underlined preposition?

   **A** to describe when animals move

   **B** to connect *warmer* with *animals*

   **C** to connect two phrases about winter

   **D** to show a relationship between *move* and *place*

**5** Read this sentence.

   > The feathers <u>of</u> the penguin keep out cold air and water.

   What is the purpose of the underlined preposition?

   **A** to connect *feathers* with *cold*

   **B** to show a relationship between *feathers* and *penguin*

   **C** to tell what a penguin's feathers do

   **D** to show a relationship between *penguin* and *cold*

## Lesson 3
## Interjections

L.5.1a: Explain the function of . . . interjections in general and their function in particular sentences.

👥 **Introduction**    An **interjection** is a word or words that express emotion, such as excitement, surprise, disbelief, understanding, or disagreement.

- When an interjection shows strong emotion, such as anger, shock, or excitement, it stands alone and is followed by an exclamation point.

  Oh, no! I can't find my ticket.

  Wow! That was an incredible movie.

- When an interjection shows less emotion, it comes at the beginning of a sentence and is followed by a comma.

  Well, I'm not sure it was the best movie I've ever seen.

- Here are more examples of common interjections.

| Interjection | When to Use | Example |
|---|---|---|
| oops | to show a mistake | Oops, I left my phone in the theater. |
| oh | to show shock or another thought | Oh! We should go back and get it right away. |
| hey | to show a thought or discovery | Hey, here it is in my coat pocket. |
| yay | to show happiness or excitement | Yay! We don't have to go back to the theater. |
| whew | to show relief | Whew! That's a relief. |

👥 **Guided Practice**    **Write an interjection to complete each sentence.**

**HINT** When an interjection is followed by an exclamation point, it should begin with a capital letter.

1  _____! We made it just in time for the movie.

2  _____! I forgot to bring my wallet.

3  _____, I can loan you money for a ticket.

4  _____! I just found some money in my pocket.

5  _____, thanks a lot. That's really nice of you.

## Independent Practice

**For numbers 1–3, choose the purpose of the underlined interjection.**

**1** <u>Yay!</u> We are going to another movie today!

   **A**   to show agreement

   **B**   to show excitement

   **C**   to show a mistake

   **D**   to show anger

**2** <u>Whew!</u> I thought we would have to stay home and do chores.

   **A**   to show a mistake

   **B**   to show understanding

   **C**   to show surprise

   **D**   to show relief

**3** <u>Oh,</u> I think we are doing chores tomorrow.

   **A**   to show happiness

   **B**   to show surprise

   **C**   to show another thought

   **D**   to show relief

**For numbers 4 and 5, choose the example that is punctuated correctly.**

**4**  **A**   Wow! That was a very scary movie.

     **B**   Wow that was a very scary movie.

     **C**   Wow that, was a very scary movie.

     **D**   Wow! That was, a very, scary, movie.

**5**  **A**   Well I wasn't very scared.

     **B**   Well! I wasn't very scared.

     **C**   Well, I wasn't very scared.

     **D**   Well I, wasn't very scared.

## Lesson 4
## Perfect Verb Tenses

**L.5.1b:** Form and use the perfect (e.g., *I had walked; I have walked; I will have walked*) verb tenses.

**Introduction**   The **perfect verb tenses** tell about actions that happened, that will happen, or that may still be happening. They are made by joining a form of the helping verb *have* with the past form of a main verb. Together, the helping verb and the main verb make up a **verb phrase**.

> helping verb   main verb
>
> Workers [had] [installed] new swings in Grant Park.

- The **present perfect tense** tells about an action that took place in the past and may still be happening. To form this tense, use *has* or *have* with the past form of a main verb.

> Volunteers have turned Grant Park into a beautiful spot.

- The **past perfect tense** tells about an action that was completed before another past action. To form this tense, use *had* with the past form of a main verb.

> Grant Park had become neglected, so people stopped going there.

- The **future perfect tense** tells about an action that will be completed before another future action. To form this tense, use *will have* with the past form of a main verb.

> By next week, we will have cleared the park of trash.

**Guided Practice**   Write the correct helping verb or verbs to form the perfect tense named in parentheses ( ). The main verbs are underlined.

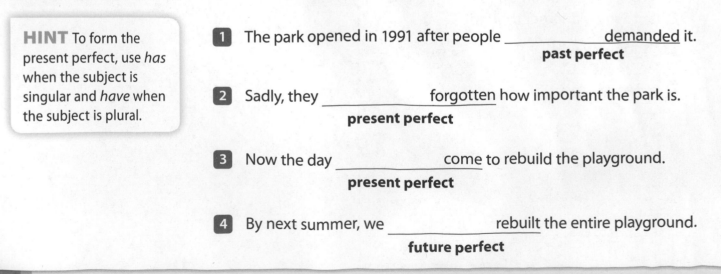

**HINT** To form the present perfect, use *has* when the subject is singular and *have* when the subject is plural.

1   The park opened in 1991 after people _____ <u>demanded</u> it.
   **past perfect**

2   Sadly, they _____ <u>forgotten</u> how important the park is.
   **present perfect**

3   Now the day _____ <u>come</u> to rebuild the playground.
   **present perfect**

4   By next summer, we _____ <u>rebuilt</u> the entire playground.
   **future perfect**

**Independent Practice**

In numbers 1–3, which words should replace the underlined verb phrase to make the sentence correct?

1. Our town will have changed by the time the 21st century began.

   A   will had changed

   B   had changed

   C   has changed

   D   have changed

2. Many families have moved away before the cleanup started.

   A   had moved

   B   will had moved

   C   has moved

   D   will have moved

3. Today, many families had returned.

   A   will had returned

   B   have returned

   C   will have returned

   D   has returned

For numbers 4 and 5, choose the sentence in which the underlined verb phrase is correct.

4. A   Last year, the mayor has conducted a survey on Grant Park.

   B   Last year, the mayor have conducted a survey on Grant Park.

   C   Last year, the mayor had conducted a survey on Grant Park.

   D   Last year, the mayor will have conducted a survey on Grant Park.

5. A   City officials has completed a report by next year.

   B   City officials had completed a report by next year.

   C   City officials have completed a report by next year.

   D   City officials will have completed a report by next year.

## Lesson 5
## Using Verb Tenses

**L.5.1c:** Use verb tenses to convey various times, sequences, states, and conditions.

### Introduction   Use the correct verb tense to tell readers when something happens.

- Use **simple tenses** to show that an action happens in the present, past, or future. The simple past tense is usually formed by adding the ending -*ed*.

| Present | We listen to music on our MP3 players or cell phones. |
|---|---|
| Past | Years ago, people listened to music on record players. |
| Future | Someday, people will listen to music on other devices. |

- **Irregular verbs** change in special ways to show past time.

| Present | buy | sell | break | become | sing | go |
|---|---|---|---|---|---|---|
| Past | bought | sold | broke | became | sang | went |

- **Progressive tenses** show continuing actions in the present, past, or future. To make the progressive tense, add a form of the helping verb *be* to a main verb that ends in -*ing*.

| Present | A radio station is playing a song by a great singer. |
|---|---|
| Past | Earlier, the station was playing another song by her. |
| Future | Tomorrow, her band will be playing music in the park. |

### Guided Practice   Circle the correct form of the verb to complete each sentence.

**HINT** In progressive tenses, the helping verb must agree with the subject.

- Use *am* and *was* with I.
- Use *is* and *was* with *he*, *she*, *it*, and singular nouns.
- Use *are* and *were* with *we, you, they*, and plural nouns.

**1** Every day when I wake up, I _____ on my MP3 player.

   turn     will be turning     turned

**2** Yesterday, I _____ a song when I dropped the MP3 player.

   am choosing     were choosing     was choosing

**3** The music _____ and would not start again.

   is stopping     stopped     will stop

**4** I said to my mother, "I _____ my MP3 player!"

   break     is breaking     broke

**5** I _____ money for a long time to buy a new one.

   are saving     will be saving     will be save

**Independent Practice**

**For numbers 1–5, replace the underlined verb with the word or words that make the sentence correct.**

**1** In the late 1990s and early 2000s, portable MP3 players <u>becoming</u> popular.

   **A**   will become

   **B**   will be becoming

   **C**   became

   **D**   was becoming

**2** Soon after that, people <u>download</u> music from the Internet.

   **A**   were downloading

   **B**   is downloading

   **C**   will be downloading

   **D**   was downloading

**3** Our neighbors still have an old record player, and they <u>listen</u> to a record on it right now.

   **A**   is listening

   **B**   will be listening

   **C**   listened

   **D**   are listening

**4** Next month, my class <u>go</u> on a field trip to the Music History Museum.

   **A**   be going

   **B**   will be going

   **C**   was going

   **D**   went

**5** I hope that we <u>see</u> some old musical instruments and recording devices there.

   **A**   am seeing

   **B**   will see

   **C**   is seeing

   **D**   were seeing

## Lesson 6
# Shifts in Verb Tense

L.5.1d: Recognize and correct inappropriate shifts in verb tense.

**Introduction**  Verbs tell readers when something is happening. **Verb tenses** can show whether an event takes place in the past, in the present, or in the future.

When you write, choose the tense that shows clearly the time of the action. Verb tenses that shift can confuse readers, so change tense only if you want to show a change in time.

| Verb Tenses Shifting Incorrectly | Verb Tenses Shifting Correctly |
|---|---|
| We went to the movies last Saturday. The movie is a comedy and was very funny. We had eaten popcorn during the movie, but we often stop so we will hear every word. | We went to the movies last Saturday. The movie was a comedy and was very funny. We ate popcorn during the movie, but we often stopped so we heard every word. |

**Guided Practice**  Read the passage. It should be written in the past tense. Cross out each verb that should be changed to make the tenses consistent. Then write the correct verb above each verb you crossed out.

**HINT** Look for clues that tell when events happen. Do they occur in the past, present, or future?

Then look at each verb and ask yourself:

- What tense is the verb?
- Does it match the tense of the other verbs?

Jake went to the movies with Mario last week. They see the film

*Frontiers of Space*. Tickets for the show that night were expensive,

but Mario has a coupon. He finds the coupon online the day before.

Mario will buy the tickets. Then he looked for seats while Jake

purchases the snacks. Jake gets popcorn for himself and a pretzel

for Mario. They will have sat in the front row, watched the movie,

and enjoy themselves.

**Independent Practice**

For numbers 1–5, replace the underlined sentence with the choice that has the correct verb tense.

**1** Ari went to the movies last Friday afternoon. She sit in the third row. The screen looked huge from there.

**A** She is sitting in the third row.

**B** She had sat in the third row.

**C** She will sit in the third row.

**D** She sat in the third row.

**2** My family watched a DVD last weekend. It was a very old movie. We like it anyway.

**A** We liked it anyway.

**B** We had liked it anyway.

**C** We will have liked it anyway.

**D** We will like it anyway.

**3** The first part of the movie is slow. The action in the second part was really exciting. The end of the movie is a total surprise.

**A** The action in the second part will be really exciting.

**B** The action in the second part is really exciting.

**C** The action in the second part will have been really exciting.

**D** The action in the second part had been really exciting.

**4** Yesterday I watched *The Secret Garden*. I loved the movie so much, I watch it again. Mom watched it with me, too.

**A** I love the movie so much, I watch it again.

**B** I had loved the movie so much, I will have watched it again.

**C** I loved the movie so much, I had watched it again.

**D** I loved the movie so much, I watched it again.

**5** My mom and I will go see another movie next weekend. We will go with Chantal and her dad. We meet In front of the theater.

**A** We met in front of the theater.

**B** We were meeting in front of the theater.

**C** We will meet in front of the theater.

**D** We had met in front of the theater.

## Lesson 7
## Correlative Conjunctions

L.5.1e: Use correlative conjunctions (e.g., *either/or, neither/nor*).

**Introduction**  Recall that **conjunctions** are connecting words that can join words, phrases, or sentences. **Correlative conjunctions** are conjunctions used in pairs.

Read the chart below to see which correlative conjunctions are used together and how.

| Correlative Conjunctions | Example |
|---|---|
| both . . . and | **Both** my brother **and** I wanted to go rafting on a river. |
| either . . . or | We were going with **either** a guide **or** my parents. |
| neither . . . nor | **Neither** my mother **nor** my father knew much about rafting. |
| not only . . . but also | They **not only** read about it **but also** watched a video. |
| whether . . . or | The video discussed **whether** rafting was dangerous **or** safe. |

**Guided Practice**  Write a pair of correlative conjunctions from the chart to complete each sentence. Use all five pairs shown in the chart above.

**HINT** Use *either/or* to express a choice. Use *neither/nor* to make a negative statement about two choices.

Don't mix up these pairs. Don't use *either* with *nor*. Similarly, don't use *neither* with *or*.

1 My parents said I could _____ bring a friend _____ go with just the family.

2 I wanted to invite _____ my friend Jake _____ his brother.

3 To my surprise, _____ my dad _____ my mom said that was fine.

4 I was sorry to learn that _____ Jake _____ his brother was available.

5 Still, I knew that I'd have fun _____ I went with friends _____ just with my family.

## Independent Practice

**For numbers 1–5, choose the word or words that correctly replace the underlined conjunction.**

**1** My parents bought both paddles or life jackets.

   **A**   and

   **B**   nor

   **C**   but also

   **D**   either

**2** We brought not only food and drinks.

   **A**   or

   **B**   nor

   **C**   but also

   **D**   neither

**3** We could either eat first nor wait until later in the trip.

   **A**   and

   **B**   or

   **C**   whether

   **D**   but also

**4** I wasn't sure either the river would be rough or calm.

   **A**   whether

   **B**   neither

   **C**   not only

   **D**   both

**5** I also wanted to make sure that I was neither too cold but too warm.

   **A**   or

   **B**   but also

   **C**   and

   **D**   nor

## Lesson 8
# Punctuating Items in a Series

**L.5.2a:** Use punctuation to separate items in a series.

**Introduction** Use a **comma** (,) to separate three or more items in a **series**, or list. Place a comma after each item in the series except the last one.

- Use commas when you list three or more words in a series.

  Many murals decorate buildings in Philadelphia, Chicago, and Boston.

- Use commas when you list three or more phrases in a series.

  People paint murals on buildings, in tunnels, and even along roadsides.

- Use commas when you list three or more clauses in a series.

  You might see a mural when visiting a museum, driving on a highway, or walking around your neighborhood.

Without commas, the items in these lists would run together, making the sentences unclear.

**Guided Practice** **Read the passage. Then add commas where they are needed.**

**HINT** When you use commas to separate items in a series, put a comma before the conjunction *and* or *or*. Do <u>not</u> put a comma after the conjunction.

Cities around the country are changing. Faded boards dull concrete and old bricks are coming to life. Communities are turning the walls of their buildings roads and bridges into colorful murals. Painters might show local scenes honor a hero or celebrate a culture.

Murals can also be great projects for schools. They encourage teamwork school spirit and creativity. What would you paint? Your mural could inspire people to recycle be a volunteer or cheer for a team.

## Independent Practice

**For numbers 1–4, answer the questions.**

**1** Read this sentence. Then answer the question.

> Three famous artists who painted murals were <u>Rivera Orozco and Siquieros</u>.

What is the correct position of commas in the underlined section of the sentence?

**A** Rivera Orozco, and Siquieros

**B** Rivera, Orozco, and Siquieros

**C** Rivera Orozco, and, Siquieros

**D** Rivera, Orozco and, Siquieros

**2** Read this sentence. Then answer the question.

> They painted murals to <u>educate inspire and unite people</u> across Mexico.

What is the correct position of commas in the underlined section of the sentence?

**A** educate inspire, and, unite people

**B** educate inspire and unite people

**C** educate, inspire, and unite people

**D** educate, inspire, and unite, people

**3** Read this sentence. Then answer the question.

> Siquieros <u>sprayed paint used bold lines and</u> splattered colors.

What is the correct position of commas in the underlined section of the sentence?

**A** sprayed paint, used bold lines, and

**B** sprayed, paint used bold lines, and

**C** sprayed, paint used bold, lines, and

**D** sprayed paint, used bold lines and,

**4** Read this sentence. Then answer the question.

> You can see murals painted by Rivera in <u>San Francisco Detroit and Mexico City</u>.

What is the correct position of commas in the underlined section of the sentence?

**A** San Francisco, Detroit, and, Mexico City

**B** San Francisco, Detroit and Mexico, City

**C** San Francisco Detroit, and, Mexico City

**D** San Francisco, Detroit, and Mexico City

# Lesson 9
# Commas After Introductory Elements

**L.5.2b:** Use a comma to separate an introductory element from the rest of the sentence.
**L.5.2c:** Use a comma to set off the words *yes* and *no* (e.g., *Yes, thank you*) ....

**Introduction** Good writers vary the beginnings of their sentences to make their writing more interesting. When you write, use a **comma** (,) to set off an introductory word or phrase from the rest of the sentence.

- Use a comma after introductory words such as *yes* and *no*.

> Yes, Victor was looking forward to the race in Chile.
>
> No, it wouldn't be easy to run across the Atacama Desert.

- Use a comma after a dependent clause that comes at the beginning of a sentence. A dependent clause can begin with a subordinating conjunction such as *while* or *because*.

> While on the plane ride to Chile, Victor thought about the race.
>
> Because he had trained hard, he was in great shape.

- Use a comma after a prepositional phrase that comes at the beginning of a sentence.

> Under the blazing sun, more than 100 people would race for seven days.

**Guided Practice** **Read the passage. Then add commas where they are needed.**

**HINT** Some sentences begin with two prepositional phrases in a row. There is usually a comma only after the second prepositional phrase.

**Example:**
Under the shade of a tree, the runner rested.

Victor was standing in the driest place on Earth. In some parts of the Atacama Desert not a single drop of water had been seen for decades. On his back Victor's gear seemed especially heavy. He had food, clothes, and water for the next 250 kilometers. Could he make it? Yes he could.

While he waited for the race to begin Victor's heart pounded. Above the desert wispy clouds crossed the deep blue sky.

### Independent Practice

**For numbers 1–5, choose the correct way to rewrite the underlined part of each sentence.**

**1** At the end of the first day Victor collapsed in his tent.

- **A** At the end, of the first day Victor
- **B** At the end of the first day, Victor
- **C** At the end of the first day, Victor,
- **D** At the end, of the first day, Victor

**2** Before the sun rose the runners set out across the plains.

- **A** Before the sun rose, the runners
- **B** Before the sun, rose the runners
- **C** Before, the sun rose, the runners
- **D** Before the sun rose, the runners,

**3** Although sand stung his face Victor kept running.

- **A** Although, sand stung his face, Victor
- **B** Although, sand stung his face Victor
- **C** Although sand stung his face, Victor
- **D** Although sand stung his face Victor,

**4** When he finally reached the finish line he was thrilled.

- **A** When he finally, reached the finish line he
- **B** When he finally reached, the finish line, he
- **C** When, he finally reached the finish line he
- **D** When he finally reached the finish line, he

**5** Yes he had achieved the goal of a lifetime.

- **A** Yes he had, achieved
- **B** Yes, he had achieved,
- **C** Yes, he had achieved
- **D** Yes, he had, achieved

## Lesson 10
# More Uses for Commas

**L.5.2c:** Use a comma to set off … a tag question from the rest of the sentence (e.g., *It's true, isn't it?*), and to indicate direct address (e.g., *Is that you, Steve?*).

### 👥 Introduction

When you write, use a **comma** (,) to set off the part of a sentence that asks a tag question or addresses a person by name.

- A **tag question** comes at the end of a sentence that makes a statement. It is a way of asking someone to think about or agree with what you have just said. Use a comma to set off a tag question from the rest of the sentence.

> This is a big game for us, isn't it?
>
> You don't want to lose, do you?

- A noun of **direct address** names a person being spoken to. The noun may come at the beginning, in the middle, or at the end of a sentence. Use a comma or commas to set off a noun of direct address from the rest of the sentence.

> Daria, I know how hard you've worked this season.
>
> What do you think, Coach Cody, about our chances of winning?
>
> I think we're ready for the game, Daria.

### 👥 Guided Practice

**Read the passage. Then add commas where they are needed.**

**HINT** When a noun of direct address comes in the middle of a sentence, put a comma before *and* after the name.

"This is a really important game Daria," Olivia said. The two girls stood on the basketball court. The gym was packed.

Daria saw the Cougars' star player walking toward her. "You missed all your free throws last week didn't you?" said the girl.

Daria replied, "I know who you are Izzy James and I'm not listening to you."

Olivia said, "Daria just relax. Izzy's just teasing us you know?"

**Independent Practice**

**For numbers 1–5, choose the sentence in each group that is punctuated correctly.**

1. **A** Lynn you're going to jump for the ball.

   **B** Lynn, you're, going to jump for the ball.

   **C** Lynn, you're going to jump for the ball.

   **D** Lynn, you're going to jump, for the ball.

2. **A** Thanks, for giving me this chance, Coach Cody.

   **B** Thanks for giving me this chance Coach Cody.

   **C** Thanks, for giving me this chance Coach Cody.

   **D** Thanks for giving me this chance, Coach Cody.

3. **A** I think you, Olivia should guard their forward.

   **B** I think you Olivia should guard their forward.

   **C** I think you, Olivia, should guard their forward.

   **D** I think you Olivia, should guard their forward.

4. **A** I'd love to see this team, win, wouldn't you?

   **B** I'd love to see this team win, wouldn't you?

   **C** I'd love to see this team win wouldn't you?

   **D** I'd love to see this team win wouldn't, you?

5. **A** They didn't win any games last year, did they?

   **B** They didn't win any games, last year, did they?

   **C** They didn't win any games last year did they?

   **D** They didn't win any games last, year did they?

# Lesson 11
# Punctuating Titles of Works

L.5.2d: Use underlining, quotation marks, or italics to indicate titles of works.

**Introduction** When you write, you might include the title of a creative work, such as a book or a poem. Titles of creative works are written in special ways.

- Use **quotation marks (" ")** around the titles of short works, such as stories, poems, songs, articles, and chapters of books.

> Have you read the article "Mountain Time"?
>
> The poem "Blue Ridge" was quoted in it.
>
> The writer also mentioned the song "The Long Way."

- When writing by hand, **underline** the titles of longer works such as books, magazines, newspapers, plays, and movies. If you are using a computer, show these titles in *italic type*.

> The magazine <u>Mountain Days Monthly</u> just arrived at our house.
> **(if handwritten)**
>
> The magazine *Mountain Days Monthly* just arrived at our house.
> **(if on a computer)**

**Guided Practice** **Read the movie review. Correct the titles of short and long works by adding quotation marks and underlining.**

**HINT** When you write the name of a longer work, either underline or italicize it. Do not do both.

**Correct:** <u>Ozma of Oz</u>
**Correct:** *Ozma of Oz*
**Incorrect:** <u>*Ozma of Oz*</u>

Rockville Gorge is unlike any movie you have ever seen. It is about a group of hikers who get lost in a dense forest. The main character is a newspaper reporter who works for The Daily Tribune. The other hikers are doing research for a book called Black Bears of the County. Did I mention that they all sing? Without warning, the characters start singing I'm So Lost I Feel Alone. Have you ever heard of the poem Turkeys Are for Gobbling? The main character reads that poem out loud for no reason I can figure out. The movie reminded me of my least favorite short story, It's Just a Bad Dream.

👤 **Independent Practice**

**For numbers 1–5, choose the correct way to rewrite the title of each work.**

**1** Climbing Grandfather Mountain is a great book.

   **A**   "Climbing Grandfather Mountain"

   **B**   *"Climbing Grandfather Mountain"*

   **C**   <u>Climbing Grandfather Mountain</u>

   **D**   *Climbing Grandfather Mountain*

**2** The first chapter of the book is called Navigating the Trail.

   **A**   <u>Navigating the Trail</u>

   **B**   "Navigating the Trail"

   **C**   <u>"Navigating the Trail"</u>

   **D**   *Navigating the Trail*

**3** During my hike, I hummed a tune called Clear Days.

   **A**   "Clear Days"

   **B**   <u>Clear Days</u>

   **C**   *Clear Days*

   **D**   *"Clear Days"*

**4** Every issue of Blue Ridge Camping Magazine has amazing photography.

   **A**   "Blue Ridge" Camping Magazine

   **B**   <u>"Blue Ridge Camping Magazine"</u>

   **C**   "Blue Ridge Camping Magazine"

   **D**   *Blue Ridge Camping Magazine*

**5** Mountain Years is a funny play with a surprise ending.

   **A**   "Mountain Years"

   **B**   *"Mountain Years"*

   **C**   *Mountain Years*

   **D**   "Mountain" Years

## Lesson 12
## Revising Sentences

L.5.3a: Expand . . . and reduce sentences for meaning, reader/listener interest, and style.

**Introduction** Good writers revise their writing to make sure their ideas grab and hold a reader's attention. There are many ways to revise sentences to improve them.

- You can **expand** a sentence by adding details that make the sentence more interesting.

| Add Details | *Weak:* Hula is a beautiful Hawaiian dance. |
|---|---|
| | *Better:* With its pulsing drums and flowing steps, hula is a beautiful Hawaiian dance. |

- You can **shorten** a sentence by deleting unnecessary words or cutting repetition. Short sentences get to the point. They also create rhythm when mixed with longer sentences.

| Delete Words | *Weak:* I'll start by saying that I think the dancers move like swaying palm trees. |
|---|---|
| | *Better:* The dancers move like swaying palm trees. |
| Avoid Repetition | *Weak:* Hula is fairly simple and not difficult because it is a dance based on just six basic moves that dancers do. |
| | *Better:* Hula is fairly simple because it is based on just six moves. |

**Guided Practice** Improve each sentence by adding details, deleting words, or avoiding repetition. If you need to add details, use facts from the tables above.

**HINT** To decide the best way to revise a sentence, ask yourself: Does it need fewer words or more details?

**1** Hula is a dance.

_____

_____

**2** Now I will tell you that hula is not just for women, but in fact men also dance hula, too.

_____

_____

**3** Modern hula today includes stringed instruments like the ukulele, guitar, and other stringed instruments that are also used in addition to traditional instruments like rattles and gourds.

_____

_____

**👤 Independent Practice**

**For numbers 1–4, choose the best way to revise the sentence.**

1. Hula dancers often wear things they find in nature.

   A    Hula dancers wear costumes.

   B    Hula dancers wear natural things.

   C    Hula dancers often wear headbands and bracelets made of leaves.

   D    Hula dancers often wear things from nature such as natural leaves.

2. Some types involve chanting.

   A    Chanting is in some types.

   B    Chanting is an important part of some types of hula.

   C    When hula dancers dance the hula, sometimes they chant as they dance.

   D    Sometimes people chant during the hula when they do certain types of hula.

3. Queen Lili'uokalani wrote lots of songs, and one song she wrote was the famous song called "Aloha Oe."

   A    Queen Lili'uokalani wrote many songs, including the famous "Aloha Oe."

   B    Queen Lili'uokalani wrote "Aloha Oe."

   C    Queen Lili'uokalani wrote songs, and she wrote "Aloha Oe," a famous song.

   D    Queen Lili'uokalani wrote songs, and one she wrote was famous.

4. Hula means more than entertainment for tourists, and this meaning is the celebration of Hawaiian history.

   A    Hula's meaning is the celebration of Hawaiian history, not only just entertainment.

   B    Hula entertains tourists and it also means the celebration of Hawaiian history.

   C    In addition to entertaining tourists, hula has a lot of meaning.

   D    More than just entertainment, hula is the celebration of Hawaiian history.

## Lesson 13
## Combining Sentences

L.5.3a: [C]ombine . . . sentences for meaning, reader/listener interest, and style.

**Introduction** Good writers avoid strings of short, choppy sentences. You can **combine sentences** with related ideas to vary sentence style and length.

- When the ideas in sentences are related and equally important, you can join them with a **coordinating conjunction**, such as *and*, *but*, *or*, or *so*. Use a comma before the conjunction if each idea is a complete sentence.

**Choppy:** Our class is putting on a play. I want to be the lion.

**Better:** Our class is putting on a play, and I want to be the lion.

**Choppy:** I love to perform. I get nervous. I breathe deeply to relax.

**Better:** I love to perform but get nervous, so I breathe deeply to relax.

- When one idea is more important than the other, you can join them with a **subordinating conjunction** such as *when*, *because*, *although*, or *unless*. If the clause with the conjunction comes first in the new sentence, use a comma after that clause.

**Choppy:** I'll be very excited tomorrow. I find out which part I got.

**Better:** I'll be very excited tomorrow when I find out which part I got.

**Choppy:** Owen usually gets the lead part. He has a great voice.

**Better:** Because Owen has a great voice, he usually gets the lead part.

**Guided Practice** Underline the pairs of sentences you would combine. Then rewrite the paragraph on another sheet of paper. Use all of the conjunctions in the box.

**HINT** You can use a conjunction to combine sentences. You can also use a conjunction to combine just the subjects or the predicates of two sentences.

| or | when | although | so | and |

We needed a dog to play Toto. My terrier Angus got the part. Angus trotted onto the stage. We all knew a star was born. Angus had never been in a play. I wasn't sure how he would behave. He might follow directions. He might just run off the stage. Luckily, Angus was perfect. He didn't like sitting in Dorothy's basket!

### Independent Practice

**For numbers 1–5, choose the best way to combine each pair of sentences.**

**1** Lori is creative. She was in charge of building the set.

   **A** Lori is creative, because she was in charge of building the set.

   **B** Lori is creative but was in charge of building the set.

   **C** Lori is creative, so she was in charge of building the set.

   **D** Although Lori is creative, she was in charge of building the set.

**2** The Emerald City was hard to make. It all had to be green.

   **A** The Emerald City was hard to make, so it all had to be green.

   **B** When the Emerald City was hard to make, it all had to be green.

   **C** The Emerald City was hard to make because it all had to be green.

   **D** The Emerald City was hard to make, or it all had to be green.

**3** The curtain finally rose. The audience gasped.

   **A** When the curtain finally rose, the audience gasped.

   **B** The curtain finally rose, but the audience gasped.

   **C** The curtain finally rose, unless the audience gasped.

   **D** Although the curtain finally rose, the audience gasped.

**4** Green lights cast a strange glow. They made the set look scary.

   **A** Green lights cast a strange glow, but they made the set look scary.

   **B** Green lights cast a strange glow and made the set look scary.

   **C** Green lights cast a strange glow or made the set look scary.

   **D** Green lights cast a strange glow unless they made the set look scary.

**5** Now nothing could go wrong. The set collapsed!

   **A** Now nothing could go wrong, and the set collapsed!

   **B** Now nothing could go wrong, or the set collapsed!

   **C** Now nothing could go wrong when the set collapsed!

   **D** Now nothing could go wrong unless the set collapsed!

## Lesson 14
# Varieties of English: Dialect and Register

**L.5.3b:** Compare and contrast the varieties of English (e.g., dialects, registers) used in stories, dramas, or poems.

**Introduction** There are many ways to speak English. You speak informally with your friends but formally to your principal. You use words common to the time and place in which you live. Fiction writers often make their characters speak different varieties of English.

- **Dialect** is how a group in a specific place and time speaks. Below, a young man tells his story in dialect. He uses language spoken in towns along the Mississippi River in the 1800s.

| Dialect | Standard English |
|---|---|
| "You don't know about me without you have read a book by the name of *The Adventures of Tom Sawyer*; but that ain't no matter." | "You wouldn't know about me unless you've read a book called *The Adventures of Tom Sawyer,* but that's all right." |

- **Register** is how people speak in different situations. When you talk to a friend, you probably use the informal language of everyday speech. When you give an oral report, however, you are more careful about the language you use. Your language is formal.

| Informal | Formal |
|---|---|
| "Bro, you can't be serious. This experiment is lame. We'll never get it to work!" | "Mrs. Taub, we're having trouble with our experiment. We can't get this circuit to work!" |

**Guided Practice** With a partner, read aloud the conversation below. Then, on a separate piece of paper, rewrite the dialogue as if it were a formal discussion between Jason and his coach.

**HINT** Informal language includes slang terms such as *dude, ace,* and *ain't.* As you read, **underline** any slang you need to change for a more formal dialogue.

"Okay, dude. You gotta get your head together about the game," Scott said.

"I hear they got a pretty heavy guy pitching today. And there ain't no ties—only one team can win," Jason answered.

"You're not worried, are you? You're an ace hitter!" said Scott.

"I ain't scared, bro," Jason mumbled. "I just need to chill."

## Independent Practice

**This dialogue from *The Adventures of Tom Sawyer* is written in dialect. Tom is whitewashing a fence when his friend Ben Rogers comes along. Rewrite this dialogue as if two friends were talking today.**

**1** BEN: Hello, old chap, you got to work today, hey?
TOM: Why, it's you Ben! I warn't noticing.

_____

_____

**2** BEN: Say, I'm going in a-swimming, I am. Don't you wish you could? But of course you'd druther *work*—wouldn't you? Course you would!

_____

_____

**3** TOM: What do you call work*!*
BEN: Why, ain't *that* work?
TOM: Well, maybe it is and maybe it ain't. All I know is, it suits Tom Sawyer.

_____

_____

**4** BEN: Oh come on, now, you don't mean to let on that you like it?
TOM: Like it? Why I don't see why I oughtn't to like it. Does a boy get a chance to whitewash a fence every day?

_____

_____

_____

## Lesson 15
# Using Context Clues

**L.5.4a:** Use context (e.g., cause/effect relationships and comparisons in text) as a clue to the meaning of a word or phrase.

**Introduction** You can use **context clues** to figure out the meaning of an unfamiliar word. The chart below gives examples of different types of context clues.

| Type of Clue | Example |
|---|---|
| Definition | <u>Superfoods</u>, or natural foods that may prevent disease, have become popular. |
| Cause/Effect | Some superfoods, such as blueberries and red beans, contain <u>antioxidants</u>. These can help remove harmful substances from the human body. |
| Comparison | Some experts look <u>dubiously</u> on claims about superfoods, but other experts believe strongly that these foods can improve health. |

Context clues can also help you figure out words with more than one meaning. For example, the table below has two sentences with the word *source*. What does *source* mean in each sentence? You can use the underlined context clues to figure out which meaning of *source* is being used.

| Sentence | Context Clues | Definition |
|---|---|---|
| Choosing high-sugar drinks can be a source of health <u>problems</u>. | A <u>problem</u> has a cause. Therefore, the source of a problem is its cause. | the cause of something |
| The <u>website</u> MyPlate.gov is a source for <u>facts</u> about food choices. | A <u>website</u> can have information such as <u>facts</u>. Therefore, a source is something that gives information. | something that gives information |

The sentences before and after the sentence with an unfamiliar word can also hold context clues.

**Guided Practice** Determine the meanings of *fleeting, empirical,* and *panacea.* Then underline the words or phrases that helped you determine their meaning.

**HINT** The phrases *as a result of, because of,* and *thanks to* all signal cause-and-effect relationships. Words such as *but, too, also,* and *as well as* all indicate comparisons.

Some fads are **fleeting**, but more than a few people feel that superfoods are here to stay. The idea of superfoods isn't new, but the amount of **empirical** information we have about them is. Scientific observations and tests offer some evidence that certain foods can help people stay healthy. Nobody claims that these foods are a **panacea**—nothing can guarantee perfect health or cure every disease—but they can be part of a sensible diet.

### Independent Practice

**For numbers 1 and 2, read the paragraph. Then answer the questions.**

For centuries, people in coastal areas of China and Japan have harvested a superfood found in <u>marine</u> environments. Recent studies show that eating seaweed protects against infection. It also might reduce the risk of serious diseases and extend peoples' life spans. If true, these would be important benefits.

**1** What does the word <u>marine</u> mean in this paragraph?

**A**  very nutritious

**B**  dark blue in color

**C**  having to do with the ocean

**D**  member of the armed forces

**2** Which two words from the paragraph help you understand the meaning of <u>marine</u>?

**A**  "China" and "Japan"

**B**  "coastal" and "seaweed"

**C**  "centuries" and "people"

**D**  "superfood" and "studies"

**For numbers 3 and 4, read the paragraph. Then answer the questions.**

Closer to home, you can find superfoods right in your garden or local store. Think "crisp and crunchy." Cabbage, broccoli, cauliflower, and kale <u>detoxify</u> harmful substances. As a result, they may help to prevent some forms of cancer. These veggies also are low in calories and have lots of vitamins A, C, and K.

**3** What does the word <u>detoxify</u> mean in this paragraph?

**A**  to move in a wide circle

**B**  to chew food slowly

**C**  to make a difficult decision

**D**  to remove bad effects

**4** Which two words from the paragraph help you understand the meaning of <u>detoxify</u>?

**A**  "crisp" and "crunchy"

**B**  "prevent" and "cancer"

**C**  "veggies" and "substances"

**D**  "calories" and "vitamins"

## Lesson 16
# Greek and Latin Word Parts

**L.5.4b:** Use common, grade-appropriate Greek and Latin affixes and roots as clues to the meaning of a word (e.g., *photograph*, *photosynthesis*).

**Introduction** English words come from many languages, including Greek and Latin.

- A **root** is a word part that usually can't stand alone as a word. Sometimes one root is added to another root to make a word.

| Root | Meaning | Root | Meaning |
|------|---------|------|---------|
| *chron* | "time" | *port* | "carry, bear" |
| *dict* | "say, speak" | *rupt* | "break" |
| *graph* | "write" | *scrib, script* | "write" |
| *photo* | "light" | *spec, spect* | "look" |

- **Affixes** are word parts such as prefixes and suffixes that are added to roots to make words. Knowing what affixes and roots mean can help you figure out the meanings of words.

| Prefix | Meaning | Suffix | Meaning |
|--------|---------|--------|---------|
| *co-* | "with" | *-able, -ible* | "able to, worthy of" |
| *contra-* | "against" | *-sis* | "action, process" |
| *syn-* | "same, together" | *-ity* | "having the quality of" |

- As you learn Greek and Latin roots and affixes, your vocabulary will grow.

**Guided Practice** Circle the root in the underlined words. Some words have two roots. Write the meaning of each root. Then tell a partner the meaning of each underlined word.

**HINT** *Photosynthesis* has several word parts. The word *thesis* means "to place or put." Look to the tables above for what *photo* and *syn-* mean.

**1** During science class, our teacher displayed a <u>photograph</u> of a tree.

_____

**2** Next, she <u>dictated</u> several terms related to plants.

_____

**3** She <u>inspected</u> the notes of some of the students.

_____

**4** "How do green plants use air, water, and sunlight to make food during <u>photosynthesis</u>?" our teacher asked.

_____

**👤 Independent Practice**

**For numbers 1–4, read each sentence. Then answer the question.**

**1** Our teacher explained to us that plants are autotrophs.

The prefix *auto-* means "self," and the root *troph* means "food." What is the meaning of autotroph as it is used in the sentence?

**A** something that makes its own food

**B** something that eats food

**C** something that makes food for others

**D** something that becomes food

**2** Our teacher told us to apply our cognition to that fact.

The root *cogn* means "know" and the suffix *-tion* means "the state or quality of." What is the meaning of cognition as it is used in the sentence?

**A** best efforts

**B** thinking skills

**C** full belief

**D** feelings about

**3** She told us to check our science books if we doubted the veracity of her claims.

The root *ver* means "true" and the suffix *-ity* means "to have the quality of." What is the meaning of veracity as it is used in the sentence?

**A** greenness

**B** intelligence

**C** truth

**D** newness

**4** Our teacher's prognosis was that if we studied we would all do fine on the test.

The prefix *pro-* means "before," and *gnosis* comes from a Greek word meaning "to know." What is the meaning of prognosis as it is used in the sentence?

**A** prediction

**B** advice

**C** feeling

**D** understanding

## Lesson 17
# Using a Dictionary or Glossary

**L.5.4c:** Consult reference materials (e.g., dictionaries, glossaries . . .), both print and digital, to find the pronunciation and determine or clarify the precise meaning of key words and phrases.

**Introduction** Use dictionaries and glossaries to find what words and phrases mean.

- A **dictionary** lists words in alphabetical order. Each entry includes the entry word, the pronunciation, the part of speech, and the meanings of the word.

> If a word has more than one definition, each meaning is numbered.

**count** (kount) *v.* 1. to say or write numbers in order 2. to include someone or something: *Count us in.* 3. to be important *n.* 4. a total **Count on** 5. to depend on 6. to expect something

> Some entries have sample sentences to make a word's meaning clearer.

> Some words have more than one pronunciation.

**object** ('äbjəkt) *n.* 1. a thing 2. a goal 3. a noun governed by a verb or a preposition
**object** (əb'jekt) *v.* 4. to be against something 5. to give a reason for being against something

- A **glossary** is like a dictionary. It appears at the back of some books, especially textbooks.

**Guided Practice** Use the dictionary entries above to answer the questions about the underlined words. Include the number of the definition and the definition itself in your answer.

> **HINT** When you see two pronunciations for a word, say each one softly to yourself. Hearing the word may help you to figure out its meaning.

In 1584, an English crew described the lush plants, friendly Native Americans, and various <u>objects</u> on Roanoke Island. Roanoke seemed perfect, so colonists from England settled there in 1585. Clearly, they hadn't <u>counted on</u> a lack of food and hostile Native Americans! So the colonists <u>objected</u> to remaining in Roanoke and returned to England.

**1** Which definition helps you understand the meaning of *objects*?

_____

**2** Which definition tells you the meaning of the phrase *counted on*?

_____

**3** Which definition helps you understand the meaning of *objected*?

_____

**4** Circle the pronunciation that helps you say the word *objected*.

### 👤 Independent Practice

**Use the dictionary entries to answer numbers 1–4.**

---

**embark** (em'bärk) *v.* **1.** to cause to go aboard **2.** to recruit someone to invest money in a business **3.** to go aboard **4.** to begin a journey

---

**1** Which definition matches how <u>embarked</u> is used in this sentence?

A second group of colonists embarked for Roanoke and arrived in 1587.

**A** Definition 1

**B** Definition 2

**C** Definition 3

**D** Definition 4

---

**fetch** (fech) *v.* **1.** to go and get someone or something **2.** to breathe **fetch up 3.** to end up at **4.** to stop

---

**2** Which definition matches how <u>fetch</u> is used in this sentence?

The leader of the colony sailed to England to fetch supplies, but a war delayed his return to Roanoke.

**A** Definition 1

**B** Definition 2

**C** Definition 3

**D** Definition 4

---

**record** (ri'kôrd) *v.* **1.** to put something into a lasting form, such as writing or film **2.** to make a note of something  **record** ('rekərd) *n.* **3.** an account of something, set in writing or other form **4.** a piece of music on a disk

---

**3** Which definition matches how <u>record</u> is used in this sentence?

Meanwhile, the colonists had vanished, and they left no record of what had happened to them.

**A** Definition 1

**B** Definition 2

**C** Definition 3

**D** Definition 4

**4** Choose the correct pronunciation of <u>record</u> as it is used in this sentence.

No one had thought to record what had happened, unless the word CROATOAN— carved on a tree—was a clue.

**A** ri'kərd

**B** ri'kôrd

**C** 'rekərd

**D** 'rekôrd

## Lesson 18
# Figurative Language

**L.5.5a:** Interpret figurative language, including similes and metaphors, in context.

**Introduction**   Writers use **figurative language**, including similes and metaphors, to help readers imagine what one thing is like by comparing it to something else.

- A **simile** compares two or more things using the words *like* or *as*. The table below contains two sentences with similes. It then explains what those similes mean.

| Simile | What It Means |
| --- | --- |
| *Noah* stood as still as a *rabbit* trying not to be seen. | Noah stood very still. |
| The *world* around him was like a *beautiful movie*. | Noah saw beautiful things happening all around him. |

- A **metaphor** compares two or more things *without* using the words *like* or *as*. In the metaphor below, the clouds are compared to sailing ships.

| Metaphor | What It Means |
| --- | --- |
| White *clouds* were *ships sailing* across the sky. | The clouds moved like ships across the sky. |

**Guided Practice**   Find the simile or metaphor in each sentence. Underline the two things being compared. Then write the meaning of the simile or metaphor.

> **HINT** After you find the two things being compared, ask yourself: How are they alike? Use your answer to figure out what each simile or metaphor means.

1. Sunbeams were golden threads piercing the clouds.

   Meaning: _____

   _____

2. Mountain goats leaped like dancers from rock to rock.

   Meaning: _____

   _____

3. The butterflies drifted as lazily as falling leaves.

   Meaning: _____

   _____

4. Bright flowers were jewels gleaming in the sunlight.

   Meaning: _____

   _____

### Independent Practice

**For numbers 1–5, choose the correct meaning of the underlined simile or metaphor.**

**1** The landscape <u>was a patchwork quilt</u> of sights and sounds.

   **A** The quilt showed a variety of sights and sounds.

   **B** The quilt had a picture of the landscape on it.

   **C** The landscape had a blanket covering it.

   **D** The landscape had a variety of sights and sounds.

**2** A waterfall gushed <u>like a faucet</u> down the side of the mountain.

   **A** The waterfall was powerful.

   **B** The waterfall was narrow.

   **C** A faucet was on the mountain.

   **D** A faucet made the waterfall.

**3** The brook gurgled <u>as happily as a well-fed baby</u>.

   **A** A baby made pleasant sounds near the brook.

   **B** The brook made a pleasant sound.

   **C** There were many fish in the brook.

   **D** The well-fed baby sounded happy.

**4** Croaking frogs sounded <u>as loud as a marching band</u>.

   **A** The frogs marched as they made croaking sounds.

   **B** The frogs were very musical.

   **C** The frogs croaked very loudly.

   **D** The marching band sounded like loud croaking.

**5** Noah <u>was a sponge</u>, soaking up the landscape's sights and sounds.

   **A** Noah was good at cleaning.

   **B** Noah fell into the water and got soaked.

   **C** Noah was thirsty as he watched and listened.

   **D** Noah looked at and listened to everything.

## Lesson 19
## Idioms, Adages, and Proverbs

**L.5.5b:** Recognize and explain the meaning of common idioms, adages, and proverbs.

### 👥 Introduction

English, like all languages, is full of odd expressions and old sayings. When you learn their meanings, you'll find that much of what you read becomes more interesting.

- An **idiom** is a common saying with a meaning different from that of its individual words.

| Example | Meaning |
|---|---|
| Ivan looked at the wobbly wheel on my bike. "That will be a piece of cake to fix!" he said. | very easy |

- **Adages** and **proverbs** are well-known sayings that have been used for a long time. They often express beliefs. Proverbs usually give practical advice about ways to behave and live.

| Example | Meaning |
|---|---|
| **Adage:** "I'll help you repair the wheel because two heads are better than one." | It's easier for two people to solve a problem than for one person to do so. |
| **Proverb:** "Let's fix that wheel now. After all, a stitch in time saves nine." | It's best to solve a small problem now before it turns into a bigger problem later. |

### 👥 Guided Practice

**Read the passage. Underline each idiom, adage, or proverb. Then, above each phrase you underlined, tell what you think it means. One has been done for you.**

**HINT** If the literal meaning of a phrase doesn't make sense, use context clues to help you understand what the words might mean.

feeling bad
I was <u>down in the dumps</u> when my new bike broke. The bike had

cost an arm and a leg, and it had taken me forever and a day to save

the money to buy it. I hoped that Ivan could fix my bike. He spends

day and night repairing things and says that practice makes perfect.

That's why he can fix almost anything. When Ivan fixed my bike,

I was on cloud nine!

**👤 Independent Practice**

**For numbers 1–4, answer the questions.**

**1** Read these sentences.

> Ivan and his dad like to fix things. Ivan said, "I guess the apple doesn't fall far from the tree."

What does the underlined adage mean in the second sentence?

**A** Ivan and his dad have similar interests and abilities.

**B** Ivan and his dad spend their time together fixing things.

**C** Ivan and his dad are slowly becoming very similar people.

**D** Ivan and his dad climb trees to pick and toss down apples.

**2** Read this sentence.

> I was afraid to tell Mom that I broke the TV, but I know that honesty is the best policy.

What does the underlined proverb mean in this sentence?

**A** Telling the truth is difficult to do.

**B** Telling the truth is the right thing to do.

**C** Honesty does not come naturally to most people.

**D** Honesty causes problems for people who are close to each other.

**3** Read this sentence.

> Mom hit the roof when I told her that I broke the TV.

What does the underlined idiom mean in this sentence?

**A** Mom thought that the TV had fallen off the roof.

**B** Mom jumped happily about the TV being broken.

**C** Mom thought the story of the broken TV was a joke.

**D** Mom was angry when she heard that the TV was broken.

**4** Read these sentences.

> Ivan fixed our TV, so I am planning a surprise party to thank him. If you see Ivan, don't let the cat out of the bag.

What does the underlined adage mean in the second sentence?

**A** Nobody else should plan another party to thank Ivan for fixing the TV.

**B** Nobody should tell Ivan about the party being secretly planned for him.

**C** Only those people specifically invited to the party should come to the party.

**D** People should keep the cat away from the party because Ivan is allergic to cats.

## Lesson 20
## Synonyms and Antonyms

**L.5.5c:** Use the relationship between particular words (e.g., synonyms, antonyms ...) to better understand each of the words.

### 👥 Introduction

Words in English can have meanings that are similar or opposite. If you know how two words are related, you can use the meaning of a familiar word to figure out what an unfamiliar word means.

• A **synonym** is a word that has the same or nearly the same meaning as another word.

> Spain established colonies in North America, and other European countries founded colonies as well.

• An **antonym** is a word that has the opposite meaning of another word.

> In 1607, the English started their first permanent settlement in North America. Earlier English colonies had been temporary instead.

• Words and phrases such as *but*, *instead of*, *not*, *rather than*, and *unlike* are clues that a sentence or paragraph might have words that are antonyms.

> Colonists often struggled to survive and not to perish.

> Survival meant overcoming rather than surrendering to challenges.

### 👥 Guided Practice

**Each sentence contains both a synonym and an antonym of the underlined word. Find each one, and then write them on the lines below the sentence.**

**HINT** Words that are **s**ynonyms of each other have nearly the **s**ame meaning as each other.

1. In Jamestown, for example, colonists faced <u>severe</u> winters—harsh and quite unlike the mild ones they had known in England.

   synonym: _____    antonym: _____

2. Mosquitoes brought illness, and water from the river carried <u>disease</u>, so only a few of the colonists kept their health.

   synonym: _____    antonym: _____

3. But the colonists soon acquired new skills, shed old ways of thinking, and <u>gained</u> an understanding of their new home.

   synonym: _____    antonym: _____

4. In time, the colony that had threatened to become a disaster like the others instead avoided <u>failure</u> and became a success.

   synonym: _____    antonym: _____

## Independent Practice

**For numbers 1–4, answer the questions.**

**1** Read the sentence below.

> The colonists planted crops that were strange to them, plants that were unlike the comfortably <u>familiar</u> foods that were common in Europe.

Which word in the sentence is an antonym of <u>familiar</u>?

**A** planted

**B** strange

**C** common

**D** comfortably

**2** Read the sentence below.

> Soon they began <u>concentrating</u> on ways to make money, focusing their efforts on plants and ignoring other possible sources of riches.

Which word in the sentence is a synonym of <u>concentrating</u>?

**A** focusing

**B** ways

**C** efforts

**D** ignoring

**3** Read the sentence below.

> The colonists tried growing valuable crops for sale, and while many plants were worthless, the tobacco plant proved <u>profitable</u>.

Which word in the sentence is an antonym of <u>profitable</u>?

**A** valuable

**B** sale

**C** worthless

**D** tobacco

**4** Read the sentence below.

> By 1620, tobacco was the major crop in Jamestown's economy, the <u>chief</u> export that outsold all other, minor goods.

Which word in the sentence is a synonym of <u>chief</u>?

**A** minor

**B** crop

**C** export

**D** major

## Lesson 21
## Homographs

**L.5.5c:** Use the relationship between particular words (e.g., . . . homographs) to better understand each of the words.

**👥 Introduction**     **Homographs** are words that have the same spelling but different meanings. Sometimes homographs have different pronunciations from one another.

- The word *wind* is a homograph.

> A brisk wind blew, so I buttoned my coat.
>
> Then I began to wind my way down the hill to the village.

- You can use a dictionary to check the meaning and pronunciation of homographs. Each homograph is a separate entry in the dictionary.

> Each homograph has a raised number after the entry word.

**wind¹** (wĭnd)   *n.*   **1.** moving air   **2.** breath, or breathing

**wind²** (wīnd)   *v.*   **1.** to go along a twisty path   **2.** to wrap something around another object

> The homograph's pronunciation is in parentheses after the entry word.

- To find the right meaning of a homograph, read the definitions for each entry. Then see which meaning makes sense in the sentence you are reading.

**👥 Guided Practice**     **Read the passage. Find each underlined homograph in a dictionary. With a partner, figure out how to pronounce it. Then write a short definition above each word.**

> **HINT** Homographs are spelled the same but are not necessarily pronounced the same.

The village was a perfect place to loaf for a few hours. I bought

a fresh loaf of bread at a bakery near the beach. A dove was eating

crumbs on the sidewalk. Across the street, a sea gull dove for food as

I watched. Then I bought a present for my mom at a store. I planned

to present it to her tonight at dinner. An old wound in my leg began to

ache. So, I wound my way slowly along the streets.

**Independent Practice**

**For numbers 1–5, choose the correct meaning of the underlined word as it is used in the sentence.**

**1** I wandered down to the <u>port</u> to watch cargoes being unloaded from boats.

  **A**  **port¹** (pôrt) *n.* a harbor

  **B**  **port²** (pôrt) *n.* the left on a ship

  **C**  **port³** (pôrt) *n.* a valve, or opening that lets liquid out

  **D**  **port⁴** (pôrt) *n.* a person's manner, or bearing

**2** "Your ship looks <u>sound</u>," I said to a fisherman.

  **A**  **sound¹** (sound) *n.* a noise

  **B**  **sound²** (sound) *adj.* in good shape

  **C**  **sound³** (sound) *n.* a long, wide body of water

  **D**  **sound⁴** (sound) *v.* to measure how deep water is

**3** It has to be," he said. "Tomorrow we're <u>bound</u> for the fishing lanes."

  **A**  **bound¹** (bound) *v.* to leap or jump forward

  **B**  **bound²** (bound) *n.* border

  **C**  **bound³** (bound) *adj.* tied

  **D**  **bound⁴** (bound) *adj.* on the way to a particular place

**4** "High winds and fierce storms are sure to <u>batter</u> us on the open seas," he continued.

  **A**  **batter¹** ('batər) *v.* to hit, pound

  **B**  **batter²** ('batər) *n.* a player at bat

  **C**  **batter³** ('batər) *n.* a liquid mixture, often of flour, eggs, and milk

  **D**  **batter⁴** ('batər) *n.* a sloping structure

**5** "Fortunately, our <u>bow</u> is sturdy and true," he finished.

  **A**  **bow¹** (bou) *v.* to bend the head or upper body in greeting

  **B**  **bow²** (bou) *v.* to be pushed over with age or pressure

  **C**  **bow³** (bou) *n.* the front of a ship's hull

  **D**  **bow⁴** (bo) *n.* a weapon for shooting arrows

## Lesson 22
# Using a Thesaurus

**L.5.4c:** Consult reference materials (e.g., . . . thesauruses), both print and digital, to find the pronunciation and determine or clarify the precise meaning of key words . . . .

**Introduction** You can use a **thesaurus** to find synonyms and antonyms for particular words. Words that don't have synonyms are not included in a thesaurus.

- A thesaurus lists words in alphabetical order. Each entry gives the part of speech, definition, and synonyms of the word. Antonyms are listed at the end of the entry.

**foreign** *adj.* **1.** of or from another place: *Anya is from a foreign city.* distant, faraway *Antonyms: native, local* **2.** introduced into a place where it does not belong: *There's a foreign object in my eye.* odd, abnormal *Antonyms: characteristic, typical*

A sample sentence makes a word's meaning clearer.

Synonyms follow each sample sentence.

**prompt** *v.* **1.** to remind: *Mom prompts me to be nice.* remind, hint, suggest **2.** to cause someone to do something: *The alarm prompted me to get up.* cause, inspire, motivate *Antonyms: caution, discourage*

When there is more than one meaning, each definition is numbered.

**Guided Practice** Read the sentences. Use the thesaurus entries above to answer the questions about the underlined words.

**HINT** A *synonym* is similar in meaning to another word. An *antonym* has the opposite meaning of the word.

Today, people come from <u>foreign</u> countries to settle in the United States. Many factors <u>prompt</u> people to leave their homelands.

**1** Which words are synonyms for the word *foreign* as it is used above? _____

**2** Which words are antonyms for the word *foreign* as it is used above? _____

**3** Which words are synonyms for the word *prompt* as it is used above? _____

**4** Which words are antonyms for the word *prompt* as it is used above? _____

## Independent Practice

**For numbers 1–4, read the sentence. Then use the thesaurus entry to answer the questions.**

---

**diverse** *adj.* different from one another: *My brother and I have diverse hobbies.* different, varied, unalike *Antonyms: alike, identical, similar*

---

**1** In colonial times, people had diverse reasons for leaving their homelands.

Which is an antonym for <u>diverse</u> as it is used above?

**A** varied

**B** similar

**C** different

**D** unalike

---

**please** *v.* **1.** to give enjoyment to: *The song pleases me.* delight, gladden *Antonyms: displease, annoy* *v.* **2.** to wish or like: *My cat does as it pleases.* choose, desire, prefer *Antonyms: dislike*

---

**2** In Europe, thousands of people with no religious freedom came to the American colonies to worship as they pleased.

Which is a synonym for <u>pleased</u> as it is used above?

**A** annoyed

**B** delighted

**C** desired

**D** disliked

---

**lure** *n.* **1.** attraction: *Excitement is the lure of adventure.* attraction, temptation *v.* **2.** to tempt: *The smell of bread lured me.* attract, pull *Antonyms: repel, repulse*

---

**3** The desire for land lured other Europeans to the colonies.

Which is an antonym for <u>lured</u> as it is used above?

**A** repulsed

**B** attracted

**C** pulled

**D** tempted

---

**transport** *v.* **1.** to bring from one place to another: *Buses transport students to school.* carry, move *n.* **2.** the act of moving something: *A truck is useful for the transport of compost.* hauling, shipment, movement

---

**4** Most Africans were transported to the colonies against their will.

Which is a synonym for <u>transported</u> as it is used above?

**A** hauling

**B** movement

**C** shipment

**D** carried

---

# Lesson 23
# Words That Connect Ideas

L.5.6: Acquire and use accurately grade-appropriate . . . words and phrases, including those that signal contrast, addition, and other logical relationships (e.g., *however, although, nevertheless, similarly, moreover, in addition*).

**Introduction** Good writers use words and phrases to connect ideas in sentences and paragraphs. Writers who show these connections make their writing easier to understand. A word or phrase can signal an **addition**, a **cause and effect**, a **comparison**, or a **contrast**.

| Connection | Words and Phrases | Examples |
|---|---|---|
| Addition | additionally, also, as well as, besides, furthermore, in addition, moreover | Jamestown Colony had a deep harbor. In addition, the location seemed easy to defend. |
| Cause and Effect | as a result, because, consequently, due to, in order that, since | People in London organized the colony because they hoped the colony would make them rich. |
| Comparison | in the same way, likewise, similarly | Native Americans often gave gifts of food to the colonists. They were likewise friendly when trading. |
| Contrast | although, but, even so, however, nevertheless, still, yet | Although no Native Americans lived at Jamestown, many lived nearby. |

**Guided Practice** Complete each sentence by writing a connecting word or phrase that signals the relationship described beneath the blank.

**HINT** Choose a connecting word that makes the type of connection specified. Use the chart above for examples of connecting words.

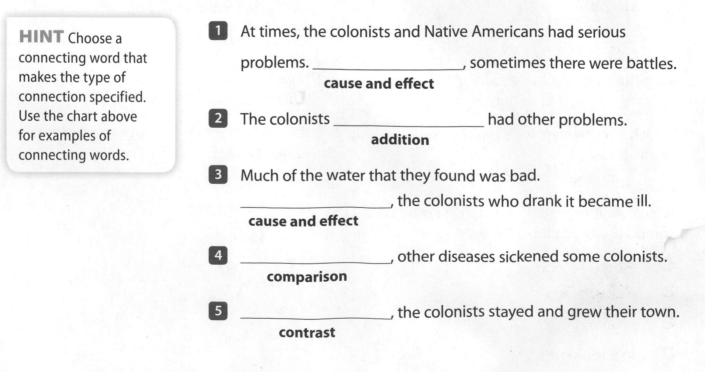

1  At times, the colonists and Native Americans had serious problems. _____, sometimes there were battles.
   **cause and effect**

2  The colonists _____ had other problems.
   **addition**

3  Much of the water that they found was bad. _____, the colonists who drank it became ill.
   **cause and effect**

4  _____, other diseases sickened some colonists.
   **comparison**

5  _____, the colonists stayed and grew their town.
   **contrast**

## 👤 Independent Practice

**For numbers 1–5, read each sentence. Then choose the connecting word or phrase that best completes it.**

**1** _____, the colonists didn't have enough food.

Which word or phrase that signals **addition** completes the sentence?

**A** Moreover

**B** As a result

**C** In the same way

**D** Still

**2** _____, many colonists died of starvation.

Which word or phrase that signals **cause and effect** completes the sentence?

**A** Furthermore

**B** Nevertheless

**C** Consequently

**D** Similarly

**3** _____, some colonists survived.

Which word or phrase that signals **contrast** completes the sentence?

**A** Because

**B** Nevertheless

**C** As a result

**D** In addition

**4** _____, they continued to face challenges.

Which word or phrase that signals **contrast** completes the sentence?

**A** Moreover

**B** Consequently

**C** Similarly

**D** However

**5** But they met those challenges _____ as people do when they move to a new place: They adapted.

Which word or phrase that signals **comparison** completes the sentence?

**A** consequently

**B** nevertheless

**C** in the same way

**D** yet